T0309224

Cognitive Hack

The New Battleground in
Cybersecurity… the Human Mind

Internal Audit and IT Audit

Series Editor: Dan Swanson

Cognitive Hack: The New Battleground in
Cybersecurity ... the Human Mind
James Bone
ISBN 978-1-4987-4981-7

The Complete Guide to Cybersecurity
Risks and Controls
Anne Kohnke, Dan Shoemaker,
and Ken E. Sigler
ISBN 978-1-4987-4054-8

Corporate Defense and the Value
Preservation Imperative:
Bulletproof Your Corporate
Defense Program
Sean Lyons
ISBN 978-1-4987-4228-3

Data Analytics for Internal Auditors
Richard E. Cascarino
ISBN 978-1-4987-3714-2

Ethics and the Internal Auditor's
Political Dilemma:
Tools and Techniques to Evaluate
a Company's Ethical Culture
Lynn Fountain
ISBN 978-1-4987-6780-4

A Guide to the National Initiative
for Cybersecurity Education (NICE)
Cybersecurity Workforce
Framework (2.0)
Dan Shoemaker, Anne Kohnke,
and Ken Sigler
ISBN 978-1-4987-3996-2

Implementing Cybersecurity:
A Guide to the National Institute
of Standards and Technology Risk
Management Framework
Anne Kohnke, Ken Sigler, and Dan Shoemaker
ISBN 978-1-4987-8514-3

Internal Audit Practice from A to Z
Patrick Onwura Nzechukwu
ISBN 978-1-4987-4205-4

Leading the Internal Audit Function
Lynn Fountain
ISBN 978-1-4987-3042-6

Mastering the Five Tiers
of Audit Competency:
The Essence of Effective Auditing
Ann Butera
ISBN 978-1-4987-3849-1

Operational Assessment of IT
Steve Katzman
ISBN 978-1-4987-3768-5

Operational Auditing:
Principles and Techniques for
a Changing World
Hernan Murdock
ISBN 978-1-4987-4639-7

Practitioner's Guide to Business Impact
Analysis
Priti Sikdar
ISBN 978-1-4987-5066-0

Securing an IT Organization through
Governance, Risk Management,
and Audit
Ken E. Sigler and James L. Rainey, III
ISBN 978-1-4987-3731-9

Security and Auditing of Smart Devices:
Managing Proliferation of Confidential Data
on Corporate and BYOD Devices
Sajay Rai, Philip Chukwuma,
and Richard Cozart
ISBN 978-1-4987-3883-5

Software Quality Assurance:
Integrating Testing, Security, and Audit
Abu Sayed Mahfuz
ISBN 978-1-4987-3553-7

Cognitive Hack

The New Battleground in Cybersecurity... the Human Mind

James Bone

CRC Press
Taylor & Francis Group
Boca Raton London New York

CRC Press is an imprint of the
Taylor & Francis Group, an **informa** business

AN AUERBACH BOOK

CRC Press
Taylor & Francis Group
6000 Broken Sound Parkway NW, Suite 300
Boca Raton, FL 33487-2742

First issued in paperback 2021

Printed on acid-free paper
Version Date: 20160930

ISBN-13: 978-1-4987-4981-7 (hbk)
ISBN-13: 978-0-367-56796-5 (pbk)

Visit the Taylor & Francis Web site at
http://www.taylorandfrancis.com

and the CRC Press Web site at
http://www.crcpress.com

Contents

PROLOGUE   vii

AUTHOR   xi

INTRODUCTION   xiii

CHAPTER 1   CYBERSECURITY: UNDERSTANDING VULNERABILITY   1
            Brief Summary of Results   20
            References   22

CHAPTER 2   COGNITIVE BEHAVIOR: ADVANCES
            IN SITUATIONAL AWARENESS   23

CHAPTER 3   THE CYBER PARADOX: WHY MORE
            (OF THE SAME) IS LESS   59

CHAPTER 4   THE RISK OF WEIGHING THE THREAT
            BY THE NUMBERS   101

CHAPTER 5   DECEPTION: HACKING THE MIND OF THE HACKER   119

CHAPTER 6   COGNITIVE RISK FRAMEWORK FOR
            CYBERSECURITY: REDESIGNING RISK
            MANAGEMENT AND INTERNAL CONTROLS DESIGN   133
            Bounded Rationality: Executive Summary   133
            The Five Pillars of a Cognitive Risk Framework   143
                Intentional Controls Design   145
                Cognitive Informatics Security (Security Informatics)   150
                Cyber Risk Governance   152

VI CONTENTS

Cybersecurity Intelligence and Defense Strategies   156
Legal "Best Efforts" Considerations in Cyberspace   160
References   162

BIBLIOGRAPHY   165

INDEX   173

Prologue

The "Open Internet" as we know it is under constant attack on many fronts, some so subtle we are not even aware of its existence. I use the term Open Internet because the founders of the World Wide Web altruistically conceived one of the greatest inventions of mankind free for the use of all people on the planet to share. In 1989, Sir Tim Berners-Lee, a British computer scientist, invented the World Wide Web, providing the connections and foundation for the rapid growth of eCommerce we take for granted today.

In 2009, Berners-Lee founded the World Wide Web Foundation to ensure free and open access to the Internet for the world's population, working with 160 organizations in 70 countries and impacting more than 2 billion people. Tim's dream is only partially fulfilled; 60% of the planet has no or restricted access to the web and threats from cyberattacks, terrorism, and sovereign states may slow a global engine of growth from reaching its full potential with changes.

The Internet has come a long way in a relatively short period of time but so too has cybercrime, ushering in a new awareness for how vulnerable the world is to the rise of a new business model: "the Hacker Industry," where the product being bought and sold is personal confidential and business data and the currency is encrypted Bitcoins. In response to this troubling trend in cybercrime, government agencies, public and private industry, and the military complex have spent billions of dollars in attempts to prevent hackers from stealing our data. To date, the hackers are winning, with innovative new tools and techniques and funded by free enterprise in a thriving hacker black market where estimates of billions of dollars and stolen data change hands annually.

New cyber governance models and legal frameworks are needed to address a world in which "hacker" becomes a common job description, some with white hats, others black, and in between, shades of gray. Tensions are rising and have broken into the public consciousness as a dispute between personal privacy and the reach of law enforcement as it expands to protect us while monitoring our behavior. Terrorist attacks in San Bernardino, California and Paris, France served as a tipping point in the debate, with a smartphone playing the foil. These events changed perceptions about unexpected new risks: encryption, darknets, and the near anonymity possible in cyberspace.

The Apple–FBI public debate that ensued from the sidebar of the smartphone epitomized a need to improve the language of risk. Distrust is a byproduct of muddled communications caused by an inability to navigate differing perceptions of risk to make hard decisions under uncertain conditions. Similar emotions boiled over back in 2014 when Senator Diane Feinstein, head of the Senate Intelligence Committee, accused the CIA of spying on its members, prompting the CIA to file counterclaims the Committee hacked its files.* Thankfully, there are ways to bridge these gaps with common sense approaches.

Cognitive Hack grew out of a passion for creating cost-effective and intuitive risk management solutions by bringing to light a quiet revolution taking place at the most vulnerable point in network computing: the intersection of human–machine interactions. Advances in cognitive computing, Intelligence and Security Informatics, and a new science called "Cognitive Security" will transform our perceptions of risk and security in ways unimaginable today. Human behavior ("cognition") is the greatest vulnerability in cybersecurity, while simultaneously paving the way for the best opportunity to build better security.

Cognitive Hack attempts to shed light on why hackers are so successful at stealing our personal confidential and business data in the

---

* http://www.huffingtonpost.com/2014/03/11/dianne-feinstein-cia_n_4941352.html

face of a massive arms race by business and government to prevent them. *Cognitive Hack* is more than that: it follows the digital trail of cybercrime to unexpected places to find innovative new approaches to the cyber paradox. The findings are surprising, as is the new science being created to defend us against one of the most elusive adversaries the world has ever seen—the rise of the hacker.

Hackers have shifted from hard targets to a much softer target in organizations...the human mind. *Cognitive Hack* explores dual competing narrative arcs: the first is the rise of the "Hacker" as an industry; the other is an emerging new science called Cognitive Security ("CogSec") as a new stratagem for cybersecurity. The book follows the digital footprint of cybersecurity through stories, research, and news accounts to put these changes in context.

Author

James Bone, MBA, has 25 years of experience in financial services, including public and private industry, managing compliance, risk management, audit engagements, and IT security for some of the largest financial services firms in the world. As chief risk and compliance officer, James has worked on the front lines of risk management establishing sustainable compliance, operational risk, and IT security risk programs. Mr. Bone has created the largest database of governance, risk, and compliance (GRC) solutions on the Internet. Recognizing the evolution of GRC systems and the proliferation of electronic platforms available to manage risks, Mr. Bone has systematically organized these tools into classes of solutions through TheGRCBlueBook (which is a free risk management online directory of risk tools and blog about risk management to a global audience of risk professionals across diverse industries) to expand insight into the marketplace for these tools. Mr. Bone is the author of several papers on risk management, cognitive risk management, and IT security and the editor of TheGRCBlueBook library of risk practice articles. Mr. Bone founded Global Compliance Associates, LLC to provide risk advisory services to organizations seeking to understand the GRC marketplace as well as the challenges faced by risk professionals in deploying the right tools to manage risk. Mr. Bone has consulted with global public accounting firms, global advisory firms, sovereign nations, government agencies, and private business on a variety of custom risk solutions. Mr. Bone received an honorary PhD in Letters and his BA, business administration from Drury University in Springfield, Missouri, Ed.M. from Boston University, and BS in management from Harvard University. Mr. Bone has served as trustee for Drury University as head of Athletic Committee and is active in other board committee leadership roles. Mr. Bone successfully chaired the Drury University's Presidential Search in 2013 and has served on the Aloha Fountain Board as well as the Davies Career Technical High School Board. Mr. Bone is a lecturer with Columbia University, School of Professional Studies, teaching Enterprise Risk Management in New York City.

Introduction

The New Battleground in Cybersecurity—The Human Mind

Cognitive Hack follows two rising narrative arcs in cyberwarfare. One narrative deals with the rise of the "hacker" as an industry; the second explains the "cyber paradox" and why billions spent on cybersecurity fail to make us safe. The backstory of the two narratives reveal a number of contradictions about cybersecurity as well as how surprisingly simple it is for hackers to bypass defenses. The cyber battleground has shifted from an attack on hard assets to a much softer target: the *human mind*. If human behavior is the new and last "weakest link" in the cybersecurity armor, is it possible to build cognitive defenses at the intersection of human–machine interactions? The answer is yes, *but* the change that is needed requires a new way of thinking about security, data governance, and strategy. The two arcs meet at the crossroads of data intelligence, deception, and a reframing of security around cognitive strategies.

Cognitive hacking is a cyberattack that relies on changing human users' perceptions and corresponding behavior in order to be successful. Common terms used to describe a cognitive hack include phishing, spear-phishing, and social engineering. However, cognitive hacks have grown more sophisticated and harder to detect by tricking users to click on malverstisements, social media content, infected videos, or published fake news accounts to accomplish the same goal: to increase personal gain through stolen financial, personal, and business data.

The purpose of *Cognitive Hack* is to look not only at the digital footprint left behind from cyber threats, but to go further, behind the scenes, so to speak, to understand the events leading up to the breach. Stories, like data, are not exhaustive yet do help to paint in the details left out. The challenge is finding new information buried just below the surface that might reveal a fresh perspective.

To explore these questions and other developments in cybersecurity, I wanted to understand the human actor and motives behind a cyberattack and found a more complicated and intriguing story than first anticipated. At its core, cyber hacking is not much different than any emerging industry that grows and evolves to hone its skills in response to changing market conditions. What is different is the rise of sophisticated technology used to exploit human behavior over the Internet in ways few, if any, anticipated in the development of the World Wide Web.

Cybercrime has grown into a thriving black market complete with active buyers and sellers, independent contractors, and major players, who collectively have developed a mature economy of products, services, and skills that are shared, creating a dynamic laboratory of increasingly powerful cyber tools unimaginable before now. On the other side, cyber defense strategies have not kept pace even as costs continue to skyrocket amid asymmetric and opportunistic attacks. However, a few silver linings are starting to emerge around a cross-disciplinary science called Cognitive Security (CogSec), Intelligence and Security Informatics (ISI) programs, Deception Defense, and a framework of Cognitive Risk Management for Cybersecurity.

Cognitive Hack follows the growth and evolution of these two competing forces through stories, research, and news accounts to piece together a patchwork quilt of the current state of cybersecurity and a picture of the adversary, "the hacker." A fuller picture is required but credible data are sorely lacking on both sides of the battlefield for obvious and not so obvious reasons. On the one hand, hackers have incentives to use stealth and deception to hide their intent and method; on the other hand, a lack of sufficient reporting and codification of cyberattack data has led to misinformation and confusion about how to respond appropriately. As the story unfolds, it becomes clear that existing defensive-only security must evolve to meet the challenge by integrating "smart" systems using offensive and defensive strategies where humans create or are not able to detect risk. What is also clear is that the marginal cost of cybersecurity threatens the "Open Internet" like no other time in the brief life of the World Wide Web. Less clear is how this war will be won.

Sitting in Starbucks, sipping black coffee and using "free Wi-Fi," I feel like I am committing a sin to not use a secure hotspot service. It is human nature to seek the easiest route even when you know the risk. However, I share this sin with many others who don't think about the silent war that is going on just beneath the surface of the web browser we use daily at work and home. The Internet has become this utility that we all take for granted because it has always been here, right?

If you were born in 1990 or after you have seen the Internet as a means to connect devices wirelessly through an endless succession of new versions of applications that come and go as rapidly as an afterthought. Those of us who grew up during the dawn of the Internet have witnessed new business models become dotcom riches or disruptive models of disintermediation executed at breathtaking speed. The marvel is that the Internet exists at all. A remarkable set of events had to come together at the right time.

A research psychologist, J. C. R. Licklider of Massachusetts Institute of Technology (MIT), in August 1962 was the first person to recognize and explore the potential of interactive computing.* Licklider called his concept a "Galactic Network" but even he could never have imagined today's advances in human communications, interactions, and cyber commerce. Starting in October 1962, Licklider was the first head of the computer research program at Defense Advanced Research Projects Agency (DARPA), which continues today developing new technologies for national security.

The concept of network computing was born as a dream to share information openly with little to no boundaries. "The Internet as we now know it embodies a key underlying technical idea, namely that of open architecture networking. In this approach, the choice of any individual network technology was not dictated by particular

---

* http://www.internetsociety.org/internet/what-internet/history-internet/brief-history
-internet

network architecture but rather could be selected freely by a provider and made to interwork with the other networks through a meta-level 'Internetworking Architecture'."*

This concept sounds fundamental today but in 1961, computers shared individual bits of data. The fledgling Internet technology revolutionized data sharing when Leonard Kleinrock, also at MIT, demonstrated that packet switching was much more efficient than circuit switching, significantly speeding up the amount of data systems shared at each endpoint. Since inception, the idea of interactive computing took 53 years to take root and flourish into today's Internet—a truly remarkable feat of human innovation!

An equally ambitious initiative emerged in parallel, soon after the creation of the Internet in Europe, with the formation of the Global Internet Liberty Campaign (GILC). The GILC evolved into a broader set of data protection principles now codified into laws and adopted by the European Commission. "In the 1890s, future U.S. Supreme Court Justice Louis Brandeis articulated a concept of privacy that urged that it was the individual's 'right to be left alone.' Brandeis argued that privacy was the most cherished of freedoms in a democracy, and he was concerned that it should be reflected in the Constitution."†

As the expectations for handling customer data began to change globally, concerns about the protection of customer privacy and access to nonpublic information also accelerated. Globally, foreign competition increased the concern of world governments conjointly with the impact on the privacy of business and citizens' confidential information. European regulation drove the U.S. government to strengthen its laws to protect U.S. customer data as well.

It may be surprising to many that the U.S. Constitution does not explicitly state a right to privacy but is included in statutory law. The GILC was formed as a global directive to adopt comprehensive laws protecting the right to privacy. In the early 1970s, countries began adopting laws intended to protect individual privacy. By 1995, the European Union passed a Europe-wide privacy law to protect citizens from abuses of their data and shortcomings in existing laws in various nation states. The latest version, voted on March 2014, is the

* http://www.isoc.org/internet/history/brief.html
† http://gilc.org/privacy/survey/intro.html

European Parliament's strongest statement to date cementing the support of strong privacy right protection to its members.

The United Kingdom passed the U.K. Data Protection Act of 1998, which forced U.S. corporations to begin to develop more robust customer protection rules to comply with international standards.* In response, the United States passed the Gramm–Leach–Bliley Act (GLBA), also known as the Financial Services Modernization Act of 1999, to develop a national standard. Likewise, individual states developed their own standards based on GLBA with modifications to address gaps not envisioned in the national standard.

The early framers of an "Open Internet" would have been hard pressed to have envisioned the clash of privacy and network computing, yet it is conceivable that steps should have been taken to ensure greater security in protecting the use of data whether personal or not. By World War II very crude cipher machines, the precursors to modern encryption, were in wide use, primarily for military purposes. Beginning in the early 1990s, the use of the Internet for commerce purposes and transactions increased calls to standardize encryption methods.†

"Around the late 1990s to early 2000s, the use of public-key algorithms became a more common approach for encryption, and soon a hybrid of the two schemes became the most accepted way for e-commerce operations to proceed. Additionally, the creation of a new protocol known as the Secure Socket Layer, or SSL, led the way for online transactions to take place."† Historically, security has lagged behind the rapid expansion of the Internet as new business models evolve in response to new opportunities. This raises real questions about the future and whether product designers should incorporate better security upfront before launching new services, as opposed to repairing the damage caused by vulnerabilities after the fact. The legacy of rushing to market with software bugs and system vulnerabilities is but one opportunity to learn from past mistakes to begin consciously redesigning security.

Fast forward: 2015 represented another record year of cyberattacks, with hackers becoming more brazen and creative. The adoption of

---

* http://www.informationshield.com/intprivacylaws.html
† https://en.wikipedia.org/wiki/History_of_cryptography

mobile technology, cloud computing, and, eventually, the Internet of Things (IoT) will continue to push the limits of security defenses to protect a growing body of customer and corporate data. The IoT is one area of particular risk that must be evaluated much more carefully. Historically, hackers have creatively used tools developed for our protection, like encryption, as new weapons to steal data. The IoT provides hackers with a far more powerful tool of attack, threatening the trillions of dollars in market share currently touted by advocates of this technology. Imagine linking billions of devices, far more than currently exist in desktop computers, into an army of drones used against us to attack with a force greater than anything we have experienced before. More on this point later but this is no longer a threat! It is already happening today and will become a bigger force in the future if left unchecked.

It is easy to discount the relative immaturity of the Internet and the inherent weakness of a technological infrastructure that has become a kind of utility that we simply expect to be on when we need it. Imagine that Local Area Networks did not begin to appear until the 1970s. Wireless networks are yet another example of the nascent nature of the development of the Internet. The Federal Communications Commission authorized the use of several bands of wireless spectrum without government license in 1985 for communications purposes.

Wireless technology is now ubiquitous, yet in 1985 no firms took advantage of this new capability until 1988 when National Cash Register (NCR) used it to connect wireless cash registers. It took until 1997 for the Institute of Electrical and Electronics Engineers (IEEE) to agree to adopt a standard for use by industry. Apple partnered with Lucent to develop a Wi-Fi slot for its laptops but it didn't catch on with consumers until 2001. Wireless technology has exploded since Apple's experiment with its laptops, which has created of variety of next-generation mobile devices giving people around the world access to resources unthinkable 30 years ago. This is an extremely exciting age in eCommerce when you think about the possibilities of increased Wi-Fi speeds and wider reception availability for a more robust experience. Unfortunately, Wi-Fi access points have also become a boon to cyber hackers looking to exploit openings presented by weak or absent security. Software providers must begin to prioritize security features with the same level of importance as the user interface; otherwise the cycle of endless vulnerabilities will continue to escalate.

Openness and accessibility between trusted users is the basic premise of network computing. Hackers have become expert at manipulating the trust relationship on the web through cognitive methods to trick users to provide confidential data willingly. "The idea of an open architecture network is that individual networks may be designed separately, each having its own unique interface (website), for users and other providers to access and share information," according to InternetSociety.org. "Internetworking" architecture is the brilliant idea of the Internet but is also its greatest weakness by virtue of how humans interact in this environment.

Social media is a great example. For the first time in human history, a generation of people from around the world share their most intimate thoughts and images with billions of strangers instantly and some even profit from the experience. Human behavior, being what it is, exposes us to "untrustworthy" links and other phishing techniques allowing hackers to gain unauthorized access to our data. The idea of trustworthiness is an important and very subtle concept to understand and one key factor for enhancing effective cyber defenses. We will look deeper into this topic later to better understand human behavior and the simple techniques used to execute a cyberattack.

Outside of the security community, few realize that the Internet has outgrown its initial roots as a tool for research, partly driven by increased commercial interests and the need for sustainable funding beyond DARPA. The Internet has remained remarkably resilient and adaptable to new products and services keeping pace with the speed of new technology. The next phase of growth for the Internet and global commerce may depend on how well we manage security in the future.

What does this all have to do with cybersecurity? Given the parallel paths, the convergence of electronic privacy rights, and rapid advancement of the largest open architecture project ever achieved, it is clear to see that notions about privacy and the Internet were headed for a collision. Sir Tim Berners-Lee, founder of the Web Foundation, whose mission, "WWW serves Humanity," recommended as early as 2014 for a "Magna Carta" for the Internet to protect the "Open Internet" through a bill of rights to guarantee independence and enhanced security for everyone.*

---

* https://webfoundation.org/

The real question remains unanswered. Is it possible to continue to maintain a truly Open Internet environment and provide the security needed given the sophistication and aggressive intent of individuals and foreign governments to exploit access? More recently, President Barack Obama and China's President Xi Jinping have attempted to establish sovereign hacking détente between the world's two largest economies. Although these attempts are tentative at best, much is at stake in how the Internet will evolve over time.

Today's Internet has depth and is more layered than many truly appreciate. There has been some confusion about the different aspects of the Internet. The Internet looks more like an onion than an apple in that it exists in multiple layers, each layer designed in an elaborate matrix of networks. Let's break the Internet into separate pieces by browser use. According to BrightPlanet,

> The Internet that we all know and love is called the **Surface Web** where we search for what we are looking for through "indexed" websites using search engines, such as Google, Yahoo, or Bing. Indexing each website makes them visible to the search engine's botnets, or "crawling technology," which reads the content in the site.
>
> The **Deep Web** is anything the search engine cannot find. Search engines index links and key words to navigate the web. Browsers are used to search websites. Search engines cannot find information in a web sites' search box unless you have permission to access the site and use the site's search box. Quick visits to Hotels.com or Verizon.com sites demonstrate the point! The Deep Web is sometimes confused with the **Dark Web**.
>
> The **Dark Web** is classified as a small portion of the Deep Web that has been intentionally hidden and is inaccessible through standard web browsers. The *TOR network* is the most well known content site in the Dark Web. Tor is a group of volunteer-operated servers that allow people to improve their privacy and security on the Internet. Tor's users employ this network by connecting through a series of virtual tunnels rather than making a direct connection, thus allowing both organizations and individuals to share information over public networks without compromising their privacy. However, there are many legitimate uses for the Dark Web including sites used by law enforcement, the military, news reporters, sovereign governments, nonprofits and legitimate

businesses as well as cyber criminals. The illicit activity typically gets the most attention by the media but accounts for a relative small portion of hidden sites. Cybersecurity experts are mostly concerned with protecting against unauthorized access through the Surface and Deep web.*

Tor is a nonprofit organization governed by a board of directors, takes donations, and produces financial reports for the public. A great deal of confusion exists about Tor and the dark web. A list of current and past sponsors includes government agencies, nonprofits, academia, private industry, and others but it was not built or owned by the government.†

The dark web and dark networks are sometimes used as secret trading routes to move stolen caches of customer data to nefarious customers who are willing to pay in bulk. But even this is an incomplete picture of the full story we will address further in the book.

The concept of "data" as an asset further explains why the growth of cybercrime has exploded. Today's cyber pirates have created a near perfect criminal enterprise without the use of deadly weapons using remote tools across the world. Many believe that the most sophisticated hackers are economic refugees who lost their jobs in the collapse of the former Soviet Union and Eastern European countries but there are signs of a new diverse cadre of hackers who are educated in multiple disciplines including business and collaborating more effectively to hide from law enforcement. The term "hacker" was first reported in 1980 by the FBI, which investigated a breach at National CSS Inc. (NCSS), a time-sharing firm originally founded as Computer Software Systems. Hackers were considered mostly young technically skilled computer programmers interested in testing their chops by "hacking" into the defenses of networks through websites simply to prove it could be done.

The term "hackers," like cowboys, is a generic term, to denote the good guys from the bad guys by the color of their "cyber hat." White hat hackers typically work inside organizations to test the security their firms have in place. Gray hat hackers such as the group Anonymous hack sites to shame government agencies or companies whose business practice may be deemed unethical. Finally, black hat hackers are

---

* https://brightplanet.com/2014/03/clearing-confusion-deep-web-vs-dark-web/
† https://www.torproject.org/about/sponsors.html.en

the bad players whose intention is to steal corporate and customer data as part of a quasi-commercial enterprise. Simple descriptions fail to explain the sophistication of technique and technology in use today by hackers with the skill to make most security defenses a temporary nuisance toward achieving their goals.

The question is, Will cybercrime limit the next generation of innovation on the web? The utopian vision of Licklider and Berners-Lee's Internet is still incomplete given large portions of the world still do not have open and unrestricted access to the World Wide Web. The progress that has been made is being threatened as local and foreign governments increase surveillance or attempt to control access to the Internet and restrict foreign intervention in their home markets.

So what is the nature of cybercrime and how does vulnerability in cyberspace threaten us?

1

CYBERSECURITY

Understanding Vulnerability

The hack of Ashley Madison's website put an indelible human face on the vulnerabilities of cybersecurity in a way few other incidents could. Ashley Madison's entire business model of infidelity depended on discretion and anonymity to protect users from embarrassing disclosure. Public exposure of Madison's member names, email addresses, and other personal information has served as a case study illustrating the chasm between the expectation of security and real-life measures taken to ensure data are not easily exposed.

Ashley Madison did use a bcrypt algorithm in PHP, according to Wire.com. Madison's use of encrypted passwords surpassed the security of other recently hacked websites even though the hackers were able to crack the hash to discover the account holder's real password. Adding insult to injury, members were charged $19 for additional security to delete all personal information from the site; however, Madison failed to delete the data completely.

The Impact Team, the name used by the hackers, targeted Ashley Madison on moral grounds, implicating the firm's business model for facilitating adultery. The Impact Team allegedly disclosed Ashley Madison created fake accounts using female bots to engage male customers, artificially boosting overall membership and growth numbers prior to a planned initial public offering. The precise methods used to hack Madison are not clear; however, by deconstructing the hack we can see the most likely weaknesses.

Very large amounts of data were publicly released, suggesting a breach of administrator access to the database or an insider accomplice acted as a whistleblower through a Gray Hat hack. Enterprise database infrastructure is a common cause of an overwhelming number of hacker attacks. The hackers raised the bar by posting Madison account data including personal identifiable information on a public site, allowing the media to implicate public figures, employees of law enforcement and government agencies, and clergy for extra measure.

One of the most frequently exploited vulnerabilities involves access to a database directly from the Internet or website using a cross-site scripting (XSS) attack. XSS is a computer security vulnerability found in web applications. XSS allows hackers to download computer code called "script" into customer-facing websites, bypassing access controls. XSS carried out on websites accounted for roughly 84% of all security vulnerabilities documented by Symantec as of 2007.* Other minor control failures, such as human error, may also be factors contributing to the severity of a hack. The exact details of the attack, like for most attacks, are not exhaustive, though nevertheless symptomatic of a broader narrative of failures at Madison that existed long before the actual exposure of data occurred. Ashley Madison was heading into a storm of its own making long before The Impact Team exposed the firm.

According to McKinsey Research, 2010 was a transitional year for private equity investments. Private equity fund assets in the United States and Canada declined almost 90% from 2007 to 2009, from a peak of $506 billion to $64 billion. By 2010, markets began to stabilize, with stock prices rising sharply and oil climbing from $35 a barrel to more than $100. In addition, the Federal Reserves' Quantitative Easing (QE) program had been in place for two years, providing low-cost liquidity to institutional investors. Basically, there was lots of cash available for promising new ventures and Avid Life Media, the parent firm of Ashley Madison, wanted its share of cash to raise capital to expand.

In January 2010, Avid Life Media's CEO Noel Biderman managed a profitable portfolio of media assets at a time when Canada's private equity business was very active. Mr. Biderman actively sought $60 million in venture capital money to finance the acquisition of a much larger firm, Moxey Media, with the promise of an exit for institutional investors through a reverse takeover of an existing shell company on the Canadian exchange. Biderman managed two similar

* http://eval.symantec.com/mktginfo/enterprise/white_papers/b-whitepaper_exec
_summary_internet_security_threat_report_xiii_04-2008.en-us.pdf

sites, CougarLife.com, catering to well-off older women seeking relationships with younger men, and EstablishedMen.com, which aimed to connect young women in search of wealthy men willing to subsidize their lives in exchange for intimate relations.

Morality, or to be more exact, the facilitation of immoral behavior, proved to be too high a hurdle for private equity investors in Canada. Biderman's Canadian bankers simply did not want to be associated with a "sinful venture" no matter how lucrative it might become. Fast-forward five years to spring 2015, when Avid Life Media made efforts to line up investors for an IPO in Europe. It was rumored the reason Mr. Biderman picked London to launch an IPO was because "Europe is the only region where we have a real chance of doing an IPO" presumably because of its more liberal attitudes toward adultery. Meetings with wealthy investors included claims of 36 million users, strong financials, and female-to-male ratios of 50:50 as part of the sales pitch to investors.

In April 2015, Avid Life Media prematurely informed Bloomberg of its plan to raise $200 million in private equity with a $1 billion valuation. *Fortune* magazine and, later Reuters, picked up the story but learned later that investors had pressured the firm to improve liquidity before funding commitments were finalized. Avid Life's growth rates were difficult to reconcile, posting earnings before interest, taxes, depreciation, and amortization (EBITDA) of $8 million in 2009 with $30 million in sales and by 2014 sales of $115 million reported to Bloomberg, an almost fourfold increase.

By July 2015, news broke that The Impact Team had publicly posted Ashley Madison's customer records and personal details and the fictitious account claims. Throughout the month of August 2015, The Impact Team posted several data dumps on the open web prompting public recrimination and eventually the resignation of CEO Noel Biderman, scuttling the planned IPO.

Ashley Madison's ambitions for growth at all costs was at least as important a contributing factor as the weak security controls and fake member counts. Most of the media stories focused on the salacious understory of adultery but the true cause may have been far simpler. Ashley Madison's story is not an isolated incident by any measure. "Biderman's Dilemma" illustrates how poor decision making contributes to security weakness in complex ways that are not always apparent. The lesson of Madison's story illustrates the importance of looking beyond a single cyber event to understand the dynamics within a firm that contribute to the root cause of a breach. Madison's hack was indicative of a failure of decision making. The hack was a symptom of a larger problem: management's inability to grow the firm without the financial resources needed for expansion. For better or worse, security is a tradeoff between risks and opportunities to grow the business. How one makes a choice between the options presented may depend on what is valued more as opposed to an analysis of the risks.

According to Dell's Threat Report, more than 1.7 trillion intrusion prevention system (IPS) attacks were blocked in 2014 versus 2.16 trillion in 2015, a 73% increase representing a tripling since 2013.* The main function of IPSs is to identify malicious activity, log information about this activity, attempt to block/stop it, and report it. With more than 88 trillion attacks on application traffic observed by just one vendor, it's clear that the magnitude and velocity of attacks represent the weaponization of cyber threats as a growing phenomenon.

Even more disturbing is the recent discovery of a massive security gap exploited by hackers that had previously been rated an improbable risk factor. In September 2015, "Security researchers uncovered clandestine attacks across three continents on the routers that direct traffic around the Internet, potentially allowing suspected cyberspies to harvest vast amounts of data while going undetected for at least one year," as reported in a Cisco router breach.[†]

According to FireEye, a security research firm, a hacker in a highly sophisticated attack used malicious code, dubbed "SYNful Knock," to take over routers used by Cisco Systems, one of the world's top suppliers spanning three continents and used to direct traffic around the Internet. "Routers are attractive to hackers because they operate outside the perimeter of firewalls, anti-virus, behavioral detection software and other security tools that organizations use to safeguard data traffic. Until now, they were considered vulnerable to sustained

---

* http://www.computerweekly.com/news/4500273520/Encrypted-traffic-security
  -analysis-a-top-priority-for-2016-says-Dell-Security
† http://www.reuters.com/article/cybersecurity-routers-cisco-systems-upda-id
  USL5N11L0VM20150915

denial-of-service attacks using barrages of millions of packets of data, but not outright takeover."*

"This finding represents the ultimate spying tool, the ultimate espionage tool, the ultimate cybercrime tool," according to the CEO of the cyber research firm. "If you own the routers (seize control) you own all of the data of the companies and government organizations that sit behind the routers." Apparently, these were legacy routers that are no longer sold by Cisco but were being maintained for existing customers. Although Cisco claimed no responsibility for the vulnerability, the firm speculated that hackers either gained access to the targeted customers' administrative credentials or acquired physical access directly to the routers.

The full extent of this massive breach is still unfolding as of the writing of this book. Yet when you look at the narrative used to explain the hack, it is clear that the expectation of security was based on untested speculation or not challenged for validation. No doubt, many new lessons will emerge from the SYNful Knock hack, and one of these may be insight into more effective ways to communicate news of far-reaching breaches in security. A "soft notice" of the SYNful Knock breach was used by Cisco to known customers impacted based on an initial assessment of the breach; however, what about clients who may be impacted but may be harder to detect? How widely should a cyberattack be communicated outside of impacted systems? The lack of robust reporting of cyberattacks, along with the stigma associated with media, regulatory, and shareholder scrutiny, provides hackers with a head start to continue attacking others in an industry or modify the attack to strike in a new way in the near future.

SYNful Knock and similar attacks represent a residual threat that lingers beyond the initial breach. The severity and frequency of propagation of additional infection or the return of hackers to soft targets is high in large attacks. Research points out that firms are reluctant to report attacks or have delayed reporting due to fear of litigation or the need for more time to investigate the root cause of the breach thoroughly, impacting timely defensive response and dissemination of critical details helpful to others similarly exposed to the threat.

---

* http://uk.reuters.com/article/us-cybersecurity-routers-cisco-systems-idUKKC N0RF0N420150915

A national "clearinghouse of cyberattack data" is needed as part of a self-regulatory system to improve the response time for events with large-scale impact. The creation of a national clearinghouse of cyberattack data should be given "Safe Harbor" status for reporting fully and completely in stages during and after the event updates on attack characteristics. A "clearinghouse" facilitates the creation of a single repository that ensures data quality through a standardized reporting regime. In addition, the establishment of safe harbor provisions is critical for minimizing adverse litigation: a standardized stochastic database of sufficient size provides a credible source for projecting trends and developing useful patterns for security response. A "clearinghouse" also establishes criteria for sharing data with law enforcement and the larger community in anonymity while investigations continue protected by safe harbor from defending lawsuits, allowing firms to conduct more thorough analysis of the root cause and thereby improving reporting accuracy. The need for a "self-regulatory" association is addressed later in this book but the purpose is to build a collaborative cybersecurity community and leverage thinking from a broad range of disciplines and standards organizations.

A legal framework is evolving; however, more is needed. A sense of urgency is felt for addressing eCommerce and security issues across borders and boundaries that didn't exist when current law was written. A Bloomberg article describing the frustration technology firms feel in dealing with a legal system that is challenged to keep pace with advancements on the web quoted a comment by Larry Page at a Google developer's conference in 2013: "The law can't be right if it's 50 years old. Like, it's before the internet."* No one expects Congress to act any time soon, leaving firms to depend on a patchwork of court precedents to wade through a number of operational cases. Examples include the following: How are classifications (employees or contractors) for Gig-economy workers selected? What protections are provided under existing copyright laws? What jurisdictional powers does the United States have over data stored in cloud servers across international boundaries? And can France expand Europe's "right to be forgotten" worldwide? These cases touch on a very small number

---

* http://www.bloomberg.com/news/articles/2016-06-23/the-right-to-be-forgotten
  -and-other-cyberlaw-cases-go-to-court

of important considerations, many not yet raised, including a lack of guidance on security and knock-on liabilities in the event of a breach.

The sophistication of SYNful Knock has been attributed to advanced nation-states, such as China or Russia, yet these assumptions may prove inaccurate as well. Hackers have become adroit at covering their tracks to their true identity and source of origin, making complex assumptions based on incomplete data inadequate for accurate attribution. What we do know is that several countries, including the United States, are formally developing cyber talent in specialized educational programs from the high school level through college and university. Experts are now well aware of or strongly suspect that nation-states have used cyberattacks to steal intellectual property and monitor certain assets deemed critical in counter-surveillance exercises. Attempts have been made to develop rules of engagement between nations in tactics and strategies dealing with cyber espionage.

A common theme in security weakness points to system and infrastructure complexity as firms layer policy and security infrastructure in a labyrinth designed to create what many call the "M & M" defense, hard on the outside and soft in the center. To explain the need for more security, and thus increased complexity, an equally complex taxonomy has been developed to help laypersons and senior management understand why these resources are needed. The M & M defense is one analogy used but many others have also cropped up. The analogies depict anecdotal solutions with no real analytical or quantifiable justification for these investments. Some of the more interesting analogies include "Cyber Pearl Harbor," "Brakes on a Racing Car," "Holistic Security," "Fortress Security," "Looking around Corners," and the list goes on. In fact, one recent report listed 32 examples of colorful analogies used by security professionals to describe their cyber programs but not one of them explains how it reduces or mitigates cyber risk.

The language of risk or, more succinctly, the lack of insightful communications about risk, creates unnecessary complexity in security response. Too often fear about the uncertainty of a risk, or worse, a false sense of security, creates contradictions in security that lead to poor outcomes. Cybersecurity is not alone in its imprecision in communicating risk concepts. However, the language of risk is a key indicator of the maturity of a cybersecurity program, with security complexity an outcome that inevitably leads to system failures. One appropriate analogy is, "If you don't have a planned destination any road will lead there." Senior management should expect to know and understand exactly which risks will be reduced, and residual risks remain in a cybersecurity program. Further, in making selections about security defense strategy, security analysts must distinguish between which recommendations are assumptions and which data represent facts. Industry benchmarks against standards or "best practice" within an industry is insufficient for developing assurance. Assurance can be derived only for a robust quantitative and qualitative analysis of credible data about cyber risks, and that takes time to develop. What we do know today is that complexity is the enemy of good cybersecurity or any risk management program; therefore, strategies to streamline complexity and make security intuitive will be more effective.

In recent years, organizations have thrown massive resources at a moving target. As soon as the threat vector changes, security defenses are rendered inadequate subject to new vulnerabilities or more sophisticated breach behavior. Security professionals are aware that a patchwork of defensive strategies is not sustainable, but implementing an enterprise solution is still elusive. AlgoSec, a securities research firm, conducted a 2012 study of the complexity of network security with more than 100 IT professionals from its global database. The findings are a very small sample and should not be extrapolated broadly, however, the results are consistent with a common understanding of network complexity.

More than half of the respondents stated that network security complexity had actually contributed to cyberattacks. Instead of streamlining security policies as threats change, new measures are "bolted onto" existing protocols, creating more complexity and resulting in human error and inconsistency in execution from too many policies to manage. Adding to the level of complexity, security professionals with vendor-specific skillsets are required to support multiple vendor systems, adding costly redundancies and inefficient manual processes.

"This is interesting considering that 95% of organizations use network security devices from multiple vendors. Even as more policies, vendors and devices have been added to increasingly complex environments, an estimated 75% of organizations still manually manage network security."* "Automation and consolidation are two valid ways to simplify network security policy management and reduce the risk of misconfiguration," according to AlgoSec.* Simplicity requires a more precise vision for cybersecurity and an understanding of the obstacles that lead to better outcomes. New approaches are needed.

To understand better how network complexity contributes to vulnerability I will borrow a concept used by John Doyle, the John G. Braun Professor of Control and Dynamical Systems, Electrical Engineering, and BioEngineering at the California Institute of Technology. Doyle explored the nature of complex systems by looking at the engineering design of the Internet. "One line of research portrays the Internet as 'scale-free' (SF) with a 'hub-like' core structure that makes the network simultaneously robust to random losses of nodes yet fragile to targeted attacks on the highly connected nodes or 'hubs.' The resulting error tolerance with attack vulnerability has been proposed as a previously overlooked 'Achilles' heel' of the Internet."†

Doyle's findings were a surprising discovery and have become more evident with the growth of cyberattacks more broadly. "Unfortunately, the Internet's strong robustness and adaptability coexists with an equally extreme fragility to components 'failing on,' particularly by malicious exploitation or hijacking of the very mechanisms that confer its robustness properties at higher levels in the protocol stack. Worms, viruses, spam, and denial-of-service attacks remain familiar examples. This RYF tradeoff is a critical aspect of the Internet, and much research is devoted to enhancing these protocols in the face of new challenges."‡

Doyle introduced the concept of the "Robust Yet Fragile" (RYF) paradigm to explain the five components of network design used to build a robust system. Each design component is built on the concept of adding robustness to networks to handle today's evolving business needs. *Reliability* is robustness to component failures. *Efficiency* is robustness to resource scarcity. *Scalability* is robustness to changes in the size and complexity of the system as a whole. *Modularity* is

---

* http://www.algosec.com/en/resources/examining_the_dangers_of_complexity
_in_network_security_environments

† http://www.pnas.org/content/102/41/14497.full, PNAS 2005 102 (41) 14497–14502;
published ahead of print October 4, 2005, doi:10.1073/pnas.0501426102

‡ http://www.maths.adelaide.edu.au/matthew.roughan/Papers/PNAS_2005.pdf

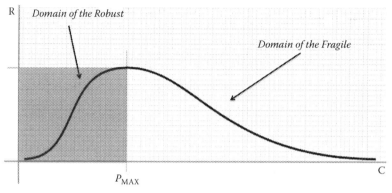

Figure 1.1   Robustness versus complexity: systems view.

robustness to structure component rearrangements. *Evolvability* is robustness of lineages to changes on long timescales. The Robust Yet Fragile concept is represented in Figure 1.1.*

The graph describes the optimal point of robust network design. Like all systems of equilibrium, the point at which robust network design leads to unnecessary complexity is a paradox faced by security professionals and systems architects. Systems such as the Internet are robust for a single point of failure yet fragile to a targeted attack. As networks bolt on more stuff to build scale, the weight of all that stuff becomes more risky. The cost of the tools that were designed to make business competitive and efficient has begun to exceed the benefit as an indirect result of vulnerabilities in scale. The security paradox is represented as the rising cost of marginal security at the point of fragility. As systems become more complex, the point of diminishing returns appears in the frequency and severity of incidents requiring remediation.

The long-tail risk of the "Domain of the Fragile" in the graph demonstrates increasing uncertainty and the likelihood of losses exceeding expectations. Ironically, as organizations build scale more resources are outsourced to vendors and third-party providers, creating the unintended effect of extending fragility beyond the full control of the

---

* http://www.maoz.com/~dmm/talks/I2_member_meeting_2013.pdf

organization. In other words, cloud computing, wireless devices, and other tools designed to reduce costs and streamline infrastructure may be lengthening the Domain of the Fragile in excess of the short-term benefits of business convenience. This observation does not mean that third-party vendors should not be used, but what it does suggest is an understanding of the incremental risk exposure outsourcing adds to infrastructure. The point is that as a firm moves further along the RYF curve, cost savings are not the only consideration. The art and science of measuring network complexity is still evolving, as are the standards and security tools used by vendors to address these exposures. Organizations need a framework for measuring and defining robustness and early warnings of increased fragility.

More than 60% of technology experts predicted that between 2016 and 2025 a major cyberattack would occur resulting in "significant loss of life or property losses/damage/theft in the tens of billions of dollars."* Others believe the threats are hype by software vendors to promote anxiety to justify new products and services. The idea of a "Cyber Pearl Harbor" is frequently attributed to former defense secretary Leon Panetta. "In a speech at the Intrepid Sea, Air and Space Museum in New York, Mr. Panetta painted a dire picture of how such an attack on the United States might unfold. He said he was reacting to increasing aggressiveness and technological advances by the nation's adversaries, which officials identified as China, Russia, Iran and militant groups."† Secretary Panetta was not the first to use the concept, which dates as far back as 1991 when Win Schwartu introduced the possibility in testimony to Congress. Although nothing of this magnitude has happened to date, it is not out of the realm of possibility.

Nevertheless, warning about a risk is very different from taking effective actions to prevent or mitigate the risk. I will spend time later in the book to review the research and development various groups have started for next generation security. Secretary Panetta's points should be reframed into a question: How must the cybersecurity

---

* http://www.defenseone.com/threats/2014/10/cyber-attack-will-cause-significant -loss-life-2025-experts-predict/97688/
† http://www.nytimes.com/2012/10/12/world/panetta-warns-of-dire-threat-of -cyberattack.html?_r=0

community respond most effectively to an adversary with advanced skills operating in near anonymity using increasingly powerful tools? The solutions may depend on how each of these characteristics is viewed collectively by industry, the military, and government. Intelligence is needed to answer these questions most effectively, as well as enhanced processes for analyzing the insights derived from the data.

A recent report by the U.S. Department of Justice demonstrates the broad impact attributed to cyberattacks. In April 2015, a cyberattack of federal computer systems exposed up to 22.1 million U.S. government personnel, or 7% of the population in this one event alone.* Cybersecurity is cited as one of the Department of Justice's highest priorities; however, the FBI was granted a budget of only $314 million in 2014, and 82 out of 134 open jobs for computer scientists have been left unfilled under the Justice Department's Next Generation Cyber Initiative launched in 2012.

Congress, it appears, has not been persuaded to commit fully to anything more than a piecemeal approach to cybersecurity. So far, the cyberwar has been fought in small skirmishes but without better intelligence it may be hard to see beyond the horizon. Recent hacks of government agencies and national voter records resemble behaviors associated with exploratory reconnaissance missions but we may never fully understand the purpose of these hacks or what damage, if any, was done.

Cyber threat intelligence researchers have developed surveillance systems to monitor activity in the dark web and networks like Tor to thwart hackers before a breach is launched. Instead of building ever more elaborate security processes, in-house security researchers have developed proprietary "spider intercepts" to crawl the dark web for nefarious behavior that might lead to a cyberattack on its customers.

For example, a security research firm recently uncovered an unauthorized Twitter account created to appear as part of a legitimate bank's customer service department. The Twitter account suddenly began to offer customer assistance but was immediately thwarted by a spider intercept designed by the firm hired by the real bank as a

---

* http://www.reuters.com/article/2015/07/30/us-usa-fbi-cyberattack-idUSKCN0Q 428220150730

proactive defense strategy to detect fraud.* A diverse growth industry of cyber vendor software has exploded in the last five years in response to demand from firms of all types seeking help to defend against an onslaught of attacks. As organizations consider their options for offensive and defensive strategies, vendor selection should be incorporated into a framework designed to simplify cybersecurity.

No matter which camp you fall into, tradeoffs between complexity and security are inevitable using the tools and knowledge available today. The question is, How does an organization assume the right level of complex layers while balancing appropriate security for its business model? Don't expect me to answer the question! The answer is different for each organization. Steve Jobs developed a template for thinking about enterprise models when he created Apple's ecosystem of devices. Jobs described the solution as being at the "Crossroads of Technology and Liberal Arts." For Jobs, this undoubtedly referred to how humans interact with technology.

To paraphrase Jobs, "Technology alone is not enough. Technology married with the liberal arts, [technology] married with [the] humanities is what yield's us the result that makes our heart sing." Jobs further described a post-PC ecosystem that must be easier to use than PCs, more intuitive and integrated. Simplicity is the genius behind Apple's success. Jobs' insightful vision reimagined how humans interact with technology. Apple's ecosystem changed the possibilities for how people interact in their personal lives and increasingly in business life as well. Jobs' model of simplicity may also have applications in cybersecurity.

The National Institute of Standards and Technology (NIST) restated [a similar] observation in a 2013 White House announcement of a [new] Framework to Improve Critical Infrastructure Cybersecurity. "Consequently, we believe that the strategy and tactics we use as defenders must necessarily focus on operational loss minimization."† Said a different way, the NIST recognizes that focusing on too many objects is less effective. However, will a defensive

---

* http://www.bloomberg.com/news/articles/2015-04-22/in-the-dark-corners-of
-the-web-a-spider-intercepts-hackers
† https://www.whitehouse.gov/the-press-office/2013/02/12/executive-order
-improving-critical-infrastructure-cybersecurity

strategy alone be enough to slow the loss of critical data? Cybersecurity also needs good offensive weapons with the capability to recognize, respond, and execute defensive strategies without the assistance of humans.

As Steve Jobs eloquently described the problem, "Technology alone is not enough!" Technology designed to anticipate human behavior and internal threats is part of new research being explored in collaboration with government, research universities, and private industry. Sounds simple: build networks with the ability to perform security that we can trust to free humans to focus on the things that add value! How does trust get built into networked information systems and what are the challenges facing an organization that wants to redesign trustworthiness into a cybersecurity defense strategy?

One of the big challenges in cognitive hacks revolves around the issue of trustworthiness ("integrity"). Trustworthiness, or Cyber Trust, focuses on developing systems that are "more predictable, more accountable and less vulnerable to attack."* Developing machines that learn and recognize patterns requires a completely new ecosystem. How does a machine become "smart"? Smart systems require situational awareness that a threat exists and have the ability to select a corrective action that is appropriate for a specific attack.

Trust may seem an innocuous defensive strategy but it is core to basic cybersecurity. However, building trust into Networked Information Systems (NIS) is harder than you might expect. Experts have known for some time that networked information systems are not trustworthy and the technology needed to make them trustworthy has not been available.† The Defense Advanced Research Projects Agency (DARPA) commissioned a study in 1999 to "look beyond policy, procedures and vulnerabilities to a richer set of solutions only new science and technology could provide." The study committee was convened by the Computer Science and Telecommunications Board (CSTB) to assess information systems trustworthiness and the prospects for new technology to increase trustworthiness. If this study were conducted today the issue of trustworthiness would have to be expanded to include a wider range of technologies associated with

---

* https://people.eecs.berkeley.edu/~tygar/papers/Trust_in_Cyberspace.pdf
† http://www.nap.edu/catalog/6161/trust-in-cyberspace

cognitive hacking not contemplated in 1999; however, the focus is nonetheless instructive in understanding the core challenge of building trust into networked information systems. The study examined "the many dimensions of trustworthiness (e.g., correctness, security, reliability, safety, survivability), the state of the practice, and the available technology and science base."*

Trustworthiness is defined as an expectation that "the system does what is required despite environmental disruptions, human user and operator errors, and attacks by hostile parties. Further, there is an assumption that design and implementation errors must be avoided, eliminated, or somehow tolerated."* Research concludes that the reality of designing a completely trustworthy network is impractical to build. Security professionals therefore must develop strategies for dealing with building trustworthiness into NIS. The challenge of building trust into systems revolves around several critical factors that must be accounted for by security professionals after the fact. Trustworthiness is costly to design and requires advanced skills to implement in configurations that might suit a large number of customers who seek to customize security in different ways.

Observations in the study point to a dilemma between market demands and increased security functionality. "The market has responded best in dimensions, such as reliability, that are easy for consumers (and producers) to evaluate, as compared to other dimensions, such as security, which address exposures that are difficult to quantify or even fully articulate."* The market has favored purchasing commercial off-the-shelf solutions over custom solutions that are more costly and take longer to implement.

To grow faster, solution providers rush to capture market share delivering products to market without trustworthiness functionality because the market has not shown an interest. Solution providers have also been reticent to add functionality that makes configuration and implementation harder for end users. Research in the study suggests that we may be years away from developing trust into NIS at a price point that the market would bear. It is ironic, however, that the industry is willing to spend billions of dollars on cybersecurity after installing NIS without the level of trustworthiness needed to

---

* https://people.eecs.berkeley.edu/~tygar/papers/Trust_in_Cyberspace.pdf

prevent or partially mitigate the risks. This is the contradiction in how humans evaluate risks and make tradeoffs in security that appear to be rational on the one hand but look irrational on further analysis. The challenge of building NIS with the appropriate level of trust was also evaluated by the study and found that a path might be possible but would require external forces to drive designers to reconsider delivery of trustworthy systems. Either customer demand changes, requiring NIS providers to redesign systems with robust security, or regulatory sentiment changes as a result of an escalation in cyber risk that is deemed unacceptable. What design or engineering changes are required to build cost-effective NIS solutions?

Networked information systems are often large, complex structures that are designed to address the needs of specific organizations. Over time, as the needs of the firm grow through mergers and acquisitions, geographic expansion or obsolescence network complexity inevitably grows, contributing to diminished trustworthiness. Very little research has been conducted over a diverse population of networked information systems; therefore, little understanding exists for improving the design and engineering of these systems to keep up with changes. The root contributing factor that enables the success of hackers is a system of our own design.

We see this pattern repeated over and over again without learning the lesson that we are the designers of our own risks. The incremental costs of repairing our mistakes appear as incremental marginal costs, when in fact these costs, in aggregate, exceed the cost of mitigation in the first instance. Networked information systems are the plumbing that connects us in the eCommerce universe we now live in, and like those of the plumbing connecting households to municipal facilities, the costs of replacing lead pipes with less toxic ones are prohibitive. Going forward, is the alternative method then the use of "Smart" systems? Can we build new applications that account for the inherent lack of trustworthiness in NIS, reducing the need for manual processes or constant human intervention? The answer is yes and work has begun in the research of a new science in Intelligence and Security Informatics (ISI).

What is a "smart system" and how would these applications provide defense against cyberattacks? The role of situational awareness in cybersecurity has garnered a great deal of attention and is the subject of new research in smart systems using Intelligence and Security Informatics (ISI). ISI is defined as the development of advanced information technologies, systems, algorithms, and databases for international, national, and homeland security related applications, through an integrated technological, organizational, and policy-based approach (Mehrotra et al. 2006).* ISI represents a very large body of intensive research in smart applications to solve a diverse set of problems, including cognitive hacking.

Recently, Cybenko et al. (2002a,b) "defined cognitive hacking as an attack on a computer system directed at the mind of the user of the system, which, in order to succeed, had to influence the user's perceptions and behavior." "The National Science Foundation and the National Institute of Justice have recently called for new research in intelligence and security informatics to study semantic attacks and countermeasures."[†]

In addition to work in ISI security other related areas, research has been undertaken on deception detection in the fields of psychology; communications in the fields of forensic linguistics; and in literary and linguistic computing, in particular research on authorship attribution. This book borrows heavily from this research in Chapter 2 to explore what has been learned and ways in which cognition leads to vulnerability and potentially new approaches to understand and address security more efficiently. This work is timely, as the marginal cost of risk continues to rise, leading to disruptions in business requiring risk transfer strategies to mitigate cyber risk.

The search for an appropriate balance between security and the cost of risk has reached a tipping point. Banks, insurance companies, and financial services firms initially absorbed the cost of security to protect customers and business relationships. But as the cost to defend against cyber risk has been rising rapidly there are signs many firms may begin to push back. The cost of liability is unsustainable for either insurers or small business to handle alone, prompting a shared approach to the risk of cybersecurity.[‡]

---

* http://www.security-informatics.com/about
† http://www.ists.dartmouth.edu/library/301.pdf
‡ http://www.marketwatch.com/story/do-you-need-enterprise-grade-cybersecurity
  -2015-09-21?dist=beforebell

Individuals are pretty well protected when it comes to fraudulent transfers from their bank accounts. Regulation E of the Electronic Fund Transfer Act requires banks to bear the burden in most circumstances. However, to the surprise of many small business owners, banks are not responsible for lost funds due to a cybersecurity breach.* Insurers are stepping in to offer insurance with a condition. Insureds may be required to participate in risk assessments, training, and computer system audits or to pay monthly for monitoring services. These shared risk models have pluses and minuses including the fact that an insurer's primary business is not cybersecurity. Yet, a model in which insurers share the risk with a small business in a bundled program may prove very attractive.

Financial services firms are also raising awareness with consumers about the need to have adequate security on home PCs and mobile devices. However, only 15% of broker dealers and 9% of investment advisers have policies in place that explain liability in the event of a cyber breach according to a Securities and Exchange Commission survey in February 2015.

The point here is that cyber risk is fast becoming an additional cost of doing business on the web. The implications are far reaching as the mobilization of the Internet expands to a variety of devices and spawns new industries. The Internet of Things (IoT) is a concept of connecting any device with an on and off switch to the Internet. This includes everything from cell phones, coffee makers, washing machines, headphones, lamps, wearable devices to almost anything else you can think of. This also applies to components of machinery such as a heating system in a building, car operating systems, or hospital medical devices used to monitor patient care. The rush to market without security in the IoT market raises the bar of trustworthiness to a magnitude few can imagine today. The lack of an agreement to build robust security means that hackers will be able to link billions of devices into an army of drones capable of launching more powerful attacks.

This constant rush forward to introduce new tech products has largely been unregulated, with little, if any, attention paid to security until consumer data are hacked or security breaches are made public

* http://www.npr.org/sections/alltechconsidered/2015/09/15/440252972/when -cyber-fraud-hits-businesses-banks-may-not-offer-protection

by tech firms. Regulators should become more active participants in setting security standards and expectations for data protection in new product development. So where is security today? What is the state of cybersecurity? To answer that question, I looked at data recently released by FireEye, one of the top cybersecurity research firms in the country, to get a sense of the current state of corporate defense combating cybersecurity. The results painted a dismal picture of cybersecurity in general.

FireEye produced its first Special Report, Cybersecurity's Maginot's Line, in 2014 and followed up with trends in 2015 ("Maginot Revisited") gathered from 1,600 network and email sensors installed in real-world corporate networks. Maginot's Line was named for a line of fortifications deployed in ways to slow or repel attack despite its strength and elaborate design, the line was unable to prevent an invasion by German troops who entered France via Belgium.

John Doyle's concept of RYF discussed earlier identified the same weakness in his Domain of the Fragile.* Caveat alert: The data are from a vendor's report and may not be statistically representative of security practice used more broadly. The findings are instructive just the same. The firms in the study had deployed layers and layers of fortress-like IT security measures around the enterprise in an attempt to prevent unauthorized access by threat actors. FireEye installed its sensors behind these existing layers of security to monitor the network of firms participating in the study, giving FireEye a unique perspective on the effectiveness of the "fortress" model of security. "Any threat observed by FireEye in the study had passed through all other security defenses."†

What FireEye discovered was a wakeup call! Attackers are bypassing conventional security measures almost at will! Even more disturbing is that security breaches are widespread across industries and geographic regions. "The new data reaffirms our [FireEye's] initial

* http://www.pnas.org/content/102/41/14497.full, PNAS 2005 102 (41) 14497–14502; published ahead of print October 4, 2005, doi:10.1073/pnas.0501426102
† https://www2.fireeye.com/WEB-2015RPTMaginotRevisited.html

findings. It shows attacks getting through multiple layers of conventional defense-in-depth tools in the vast majority of deployments."*

Before diving into the results, it's important to explain how FireEye conducted the study. FireEye examined data from 1,214 security deployments over two overlapping six-month test periods, comparing the change from the first test. The findings were conclusive, with a particular focus on advanced persistent threat (APT) actors.

APT attacks are not your run of the mill hacks. APT actors may receive direction and support from a national government and, as the name implies, are the most tenacious users of a wide range of tactics and tools in the pursuit of their attack. APT malware is also very stealthy, allowing actors to cloak their actions and, in many cases, their identity. The presence of APT malware does not mean it is being directed by an APT actor but its presence demonstrates the sophistication of the attacker. APT malware is identified with the subtype, "APT," such as BACKDOOR.APT. GH0STRAT. Now for the results.

Brief Summary of Results

"Ninety-six percent of systems across multiple industry types were breached and twenty-seven percent of the breaches involved malware."* The following data represent percentage breaches by industry verticals participating in the FireEye study: 100% in Legal, 30% in Retail, 29% in Auto & Transportation, 28% in Entertainment & Media, 37% in Healthcare & Pharmaceuticals, 30% in Services & Consulting, and 32% in High Tech.

Attacks are increasingly focused on compromising systems through the use of advanced malware. Figure 1.2 gives a breakdown: in short, 96 out of 100 attacks were successful even with layers and layers of security in place! Security defenses were ineffective but not for the reason one would think. Instead, hackers simply found more effective ways to bypass the defenses that were in place. One commonality among all industries is the "attack vector," meaning hackers, at least in this study, have concentrated their efforts on two parts of the fortified infrastructure to deliver their malware.

---

* https://www2.fireeye.com/WEB-2015RPTMaginotRevisited.html

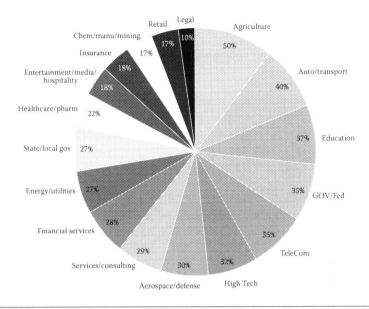

Figure 1.2 Percent of individual industries with advanced malware concentration.

Email and web traffic were cited as the most common and effective ways used to deliver attacks. Social media and malvertisement must now be included as high growth delivery channels, suggesting the problem is spreading. Either the user's web browser was compromised or the attack involved the use of APT malware to trick email users into opening an infected document. Why try to defeat security defenses when the hacker can so easily trick you into providing access to the enterprise? The truth is that the most successful cyberattacks use simple approaches. Cognitive hacks are effective—using a variety of media—with low-cost tactics, yielding tremendous results. In some cases, a form of "crowd-sourcing" for malware has evolved in the deep web, allowing hackers to create more sophisticated versions of successful tools for new attacks rendering defenses useless.

Motivated enemies have exploited human behavior since before the Trojan War to defeat the defenses of its adversaries. It seems not much has changed except the tools used to execute the means to the end. We (humans) are the weak link in Maginot's Line! Recognizing the root cause of the problem is the first step in finding new solutions. Fortunately, a great deal of pioneering work is being conducted to expand our understanding of the role "situational awareness" or cognition contributes to cyber vulnerabilities.

Returning to the final insights in the study, several industry types experienced a higher concentration of breaches. The following industry types were breached 100% of the time: Agriculture, Auto/Transportation, Education, Healthcare/Pharm, and Retail. Ninety percent of all industries in the study experienced one or more breaches except Aerospace and Defense, which recorded a breach 76% of the time. While these results indicate a high level of failure, they demonstrate these industries have either hardened security or attackers have simply been less successful for reasons not identified in the study.

These findings may not be extrapolated uniformly as a benchmark but are informative nonetheless. The FireEye test can serve as a proxy for thinking about cybersecurity and is instructive in evaluating assumptions about security in general. So far, we have taken a very broad brush to explain a nuanced problem, ignoring for a moment that the details help to paint a more complete picture. We will get to the data as we continue to track the digital footprint of cyberattacks. Let's now turn to the subjects of cognition, machine learning, artificial intelligence, and new research in trustworthiness in cyberspace.

References

Cybenko, G., Giani, A., and Thompson, P., "Cognitive Hacking and the Value of Information," Workshop on Economics and Information Security, May 16–17, 2002, Berkeley, California, 24, 2002a.

Cybenko, G., Giani, A., and Thompson, P., "Cognitive Hacking: A Battle for the Mind," *IEEE Computer*, 35(8), 2002b, 50–56.

Mehrotra, S., Zeng, D. D., and Chen, H. (Eds.), IEEE International Conference on Intelligence and Security Informatics, ISI 2006, San Diego, CA, USA, May 23–24, 2006. http://www.springer.com/us/book/9783540344780.

2

Cognitive Behavior

Advances in Situational Awareness

Only amateurs attack machines; professionals target people.

Bruce Schneier (2000)

Just as military battles are no longer fought in trenches, with massive armored vehicles clashing in open fields, cyberwars are transforming the battlespace of the future.* In military parlance, the introduction of urban fighters and mobile targets changed how proxy wars are fought. Asymmetric in execution, military leaders had to adapt to unconventional tactics in response to new threats. Cyber risk is also three dimensional in a digital sense. The first dimension is advanced technology, followed by cognitive hacks, with the end result being real collateral damage in time, expense, and reputation.

In Chapter 1, we discussed the inherent weakness in building "Maginot Lines" to defend the fort with layers upon layers of security protocols that have proven ineffective in preventing attack. The question remains: If not some form of Maginot Lines, what has proven more effective? I explore that question by summarizing research findings and asking more questions that remain unanswered. However, as the costs to defend and mitigate attacks escalate, senior management will demand ways to slow or lower the cost of cybersecurity.

How will security professionals respond? What new approaches are available to improve security and lower the cost of defending the fortress? Firms must consider new ways to address the asymmetric nature of cyberattacks using their own toolkit of asymmetric defenses. One such set of new tools being explored by the military, government agencies, and a host of industries is the domain of human behavior and cognitive sciences.

---

* http://news.usni.org/2012/10/14/asymmetric-nature-cyber-warfare

A subset of these disciplines includes Cyber Situational Awareness, Cyber Hacking and Intelligence and Security Informatics, Cognitive Hacking, Ontology Mapping, Semantic Architecture, Prospect Theory–Cognitive Bias and Heuristics, and others. Each of these areas reflects exhaustive scientific research beyond the scope of this book but deserves a mention to demonstrate the progress made to date. Much of the new research in cybersecurity is in the early stage of development and no one subject should be considered a panacea as a whole.

One thing that is becoming clear is that human behavior and cognition will play a central role in advancing the practice of cybersecurity. I would not do justice to cover each of these disciplines in-depth at this time, nor was it the intention to do so. The goal of *Cognitive Hack* is to introduce readers to the evolution of emerging technologies, many in very early stage of development, being considered to address what some believe to be the weakest link in cybersecurity— the human mind. The remainder of the book will expand on cognitive hacking and other semantic attacks.

The additional disciplinary topics should be covered separately as an in-depth analysis to expand the understanding of how these technologies will be arrayed in combating cyber risks. Cognitive hacking and semantic attacks are currently two of the most commonly used tools of the hacker trade but by no means the only tools. The goal then is to make readers aware of emerging new disciplines in cybersecurity with the understanding that the field is very wide in topical research but somewhat shallow in application at this time.

It is also important to point out that each of these topics requires singular attention to understand them fully. It is my intention to introduce readers to a more thorough analysis of these disciplines as the opportunity presents itself and desire is demonstrated for more details. The goal here is to demonstrate how security is evolving and to develop a process for governance and a framework for operationalizing a cognitive risk program inclusive of advanced technologies as they emerge and practical steps for understanding risk beyond today's simplistic and qualitative approach to risk assessment. I may, at times, use the terms cognitive hack and semantic attack interchangeably. The distinctions are slight, with cognitive hack referencing a broader range of tactics used by hackers to change or trick the user's behavior and semantic attacks to depict the use of written text and a range of deceptive communications to accomplish the same goal.

Cyber situational awareness is the hottest new buzzword in cybersecurity and the subject of new research on the role cognition contributes, negatively or positively, to cybersecurity. Although the term situational awareness is an old concept to describe something we do instinctually, nonetheless there are subtleties embedded in the definition that are unique to cybersecurity.

What is situational awareness? Situation awareness is defined as "the perception of environmental elements with respect to time or space, the comprehension of their meaning, and the projection of their status after some variable has changed, such as time, or some other variable, such as a predetermined event."* "It is also a field of study concerned with understanding the environment critical to decision makers in complex, dynamic areas from aviation, air traffic control, ship navigation, power plant operations, military command and control, and emergency services such as firefighting and policing to more ordinary but nevertheless complex tasks such as driving an automobile or riding a bicycle."* The National Institute of Standards and Technology (NIST), an internationally accepted standard on IT security, has also advocated for and developed a framework of continuous monitoring to provide security analysts with situational awareness. See Figure 2.1.

Situational awareness is not a new concept, "the concept has roots in the history of military theory†—it is recognizable in Sun Tzu's *The Art of War*,‡ for instance. The term itself can be traced also to World War I,§ "where it was recognized as a crucial component for crews in military aircraft." The term was first used in the 1990s by the U.S. Air Force; its pilots returning from successfully runs attributed their success to having good situational awareness over their opponents. Pilots suggested their survival in dogfights typically amounted to observing the opponent and reacting within seconds before the other pilot anticipated their own action. Col. John Boyd, ace USAF pilot

---

* https://en.wikipedia.org/wiki/Situation_awareness
† https://en.wikipedia.org/wiki/Military_theory
‡ https://en.wikipedia.org/wiki/The_Art_of_War
§ https://en.wikipedia.org/wiki/World_War_I

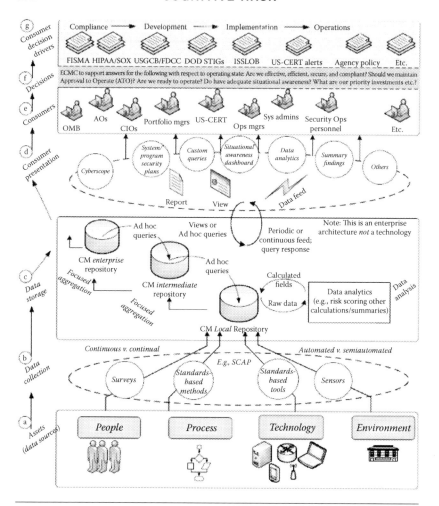

Figure 2.1   Diagram of the elements of "Continuous Monitoring" in the NIST IR 7756 draft.

and war theorist, described the "observe" and "orient" part of situational awareness as a factor in the development of the Boyd Loop or Observe-Orient-Decide-Act Loop. If a pilot lost situational awareness in battle, he was considered "out of the loop."

"It is important to distinguish the term situation awareness (Endsley, 1988a,b), as a state of knowledge, from the processes used to achieve that state.* These processes, which may vary widely among individuals and contexts, will be referred to as situational assessment or the process of achieving, acquiring, or maintaining SA." Thus, in

---

* https://en.wikipedia.org/wiki/Situation_awareness#cite_note-20

brief, *situational awareness* is viewed as "a state of knowledge," and *situational assessment* as "the processes" used to achieve that knowledge. Note that the processes of situational assessment not only produce situational awareness, but they also drive those same processes in a recurrent fashion. For example, one's current awareness can determine what one pays attention to next and how one interprets the information perceived (Endsley, 1988a,b). Situational Awareness Global Assessment Technique (SAGAT).*

Situational awareness is a mental model for sensemaking under uncertain conditions but how does one operationalize situational awareness? "Situation awareness is about the knowledge state that's achieved—either knowledge of current data elements, or inferences drawn from these data, or predictions that can be made using these inferences. In contrast, sensemaking is about the process of achieving these kinds of outcomes, the strategies, and the barriers encountered."†

To understand better what this means we need to break the definition down into simpler terms. MITRE, a government contract vendor who specializes in cybersecurity, describes the processes involved in cyber situational awareness as a framework. "Comprehensive cyber situation awareness involves three key areas: computing and network components, threat information, and mission dependencies." Put more simply, business and government leaders must anticipate what might happen to their systems and develop effective countermeasures to protect their mission-critical applications.

If this sounds like common sense masquerading as "consultant-speak" you would not be alone in thinking it's another fad destined for the dustbin of good intentions. But before you dismiss this concept out of hand, I would ask that you suspend disbelief for now and consider the data we have covered so far. No doubt you personally have experience with clicking on a link with a virus or had to mitigate a security exposure due to poor judgment by yourself or a colleague.

Situational awareness is the basis for automating analytical models in cybersecurity programs to anticipate and address cyberattacks more effectively. Situational awareness provides a framework for recognizing when the environment deviates from expectations and formulates

* http://ieeexplore.ieee.org/xpl/articleDetails.jsp?reload=true&arnumber=195097
† https://en.wikipedia.org/wiki/Situation_awareness#cite_note-28

a set of actions to be taken in response to a perceived threat or change in dynamics.

"A loss of situational awareness has been identified as a root cause for human errors in judgment or delayed response to threats in the theater of operation." Behavioral economists, research psychologists, and other scientists have helped to shed light on how simple it is to lose sight of situational awareness. Daniel Kahneman and Amos Tversky's Prospect theory is now widely accepted reading for understanding decision making under uncertain conditions. Prospect theory helps explain the mental mechanics for how and why we are more prone to make mistakes of judgment when faced with incomplete information.

Kahneman and Tversky (2000) described their original theory as being "concerned with the behavior of decision makers who face a choice between two alternatives." The definition in the original text is: "Decision making under risk can be viewed as a choice between prospects or gambles." Decisions subject to risk are deemed to signify a choice between alternative actions, which are associated with particular probabilities (prospects) or gambles." What Kahneman and Tversky learned is that we lack the tools to choose consistently among options involving probability when the outcomes are less certain (Goldberg and von Nitzsch, 2001, p. 62). Prospect theory provides a broader framework for understanding cognitive bias and heuristics as well as how uncertainty leads us astray.

Think of situational awareness as the techniques to *not* send an invitation that prompts an attack but, if attacked, to initiate robust countermeasures in response. Why phrase it this way? "Libicki first characterized attacks on computer systems in the context of information warfare as being physical, syntactic, and semantic, where software agents were misled by misinformation deliberately fed by an adversary."[*][†]

The framework for situational awareness is a fusion of concepts borrowed from war theorists from the navy and air force. Officers from the U.S. Air Force are credited with developing the "Observe–Orient–Decide–Act" Loop (OODA Loop). The OODA Loop formally defined the foundational processes for situation awareness required in successful aerial combat missions. OODA has since been

---

[*] http://www.ists.dartmouth.edu/library/77.pdf reference for Libicki quote
[†] https://www.schneier.com/crypto-gram/archives/2000/1015.html

refined into a more elaborate framework for situational awareness over time as more sophisticated applications have evolved. The cognitive processes involved in situational awareness are situational understanding, situational assessment, mental models, and sensemaking. It's important to unpack each process to clarify how the integration of each step leads to effective situational awareness.

Situational understanding is the "so what" of the cumulative data and information gathering applied to the analysis and judgment of observations in the operational theater. Situational understanding encompasses the first step, "Observe," in the OODA Loop. *Situational assessment* represents the "Orient" processes used to gain knowledge about the environment. These processes may be quantitative and/or qualitative and include data from external sources to supplement or fill in gaps in knowledge.

Situational assessment is used to build mental models representing experiential learning, expertise, and intuition used to assess the environment and make an appropriate selection among possible scenarios presented in the theater. *Mental models* represent the next step, "Decide," in the OODA Loop.

Mental models create a set of behavioral responses to the possible scenarios observed. The purpose of a formalized mental model is to the shorten reaction time in various threat scenarios while reducing the possibility of judgment error.

Finally, *sensemaking* is the process of identifying patterns in the data or knowledge gathered to choose an appropriate course of actions. Sensemaking represents the final step, "Act," in the OODA Loop and serves to confirm the response decision. The OODA Loop is not static. Depending on the complexity of the situation, several rounds of analysis may be required to come to a reasonable conclusion.

What are the practical applications of situational awareness in cybersecurity? One way to better understand a real-time example of situational awareness is to look at the backstory of the cyberattack on Target department stores between Thanksgiving and Black Friday's holiday shopping season in 2013. Allegedly, a teenage hacker using the code name Ree4 modified "run-of-the-mill" malware, renaming it "BlackPOS," and sold the malicious code to eastern European cybercriminals. Instead of attacking Target directly, hackers sent malware-laced emails in a "spear phishing" attack to a third-party vendor with access to Target's network. Once the hackers had access to vendor credentials, entry to Target appeared to come from a trusted source.

Once the hacker gained access to Target's network and its point of sales (POS) systems the malware waited to launch its attack. Between November 15 and 28, the hackers gained access to a small number of cash registers in Target stores and used this time to test their POS malware. By the end of November, the hackers had captured control of virtually all of Target's POS devices, collecting customer card data and transaction activity through December 2013.

The BlackPOS virus was identified as one of several POS malware attacks during the same holiday season. The method and scale of the attack on Target stood out owing to its design, making its data manipulations extremely hard to detect. The BlackPOS malware also exhibited other distinguishing behavior not seen before in that it made copies of the stolen data and stored the records on Target's own servers. To mask the attack further, the malware did not operate around the clock but limited its activity to the store's prime times between 10:00 am and 5:00 pm. The *New York Times* reported that the company was vulnerable to the cyberattack because its systems were "astonishingly open—lacking the virtual walls and motion detectors found in secure networks like many banks."*

Was the sophistication and unique nature of the BlackPOS malware an appropriate test for situational awareness? How would situational awareness been helpful in detecting this devastating attack? Target maintained an extensive cybersecurity team that reportedly was well versed in addressing targeted attacks frequented on retailers. According to a Bloomberg article in March 2014, Target had installed monitoring devices from FireEye, a top cybersecurity firm, six months prior to the attack. Target's security team in Bangalore, India was alerted of a November 30 theft of customer data and the Bangalore security team notified security specialists in the United States, but then nothing happened.†

---

* http://www.nytimes.com/2014/01/18/business/a-sneaky-path-into-target-customers-wallets.html?_r=2

† http://www.bloomberg.com/bw/articles/2014-03-13/target-missed-alarms-in-epic-hack-of-credit-card-data

Under testimony before Congress, Target testified that it was unaware of the theft until notified by the U.S. Department of Justice, prompting an investigation that led to the discovery of the alerts that had gone unaddressed in its computer logs. What is clear is that the opportunity for exercising situational awareness was missed if the security analyst's alerts were overlooked or delayed for inexplicable reasons. Cybersecurity professionals are constantly under the gun and must prioritize their time and resources for high target threats. After the fact, the omission was a damning indictment of poor situational awareness.

Pointing out missed opportunities is easy after the fact but a broad brush does not fully explain the challenges and issues faced by Target's security team. Hackers have become increasingly astute at exploiting cognitive blind spots by using very simple tricks to cover their tracks. Take into account the novelty of the BlackPOS malware and the entry point through a third-party provider; the cloaking behaviors used by the virus made it a challenge for early detection.

The lesson here is that an organization with formal security processes will find additional benefits by augmenting situational awareness and response in support of the security team. The security team in India performed its job but may have represented one of a larger number of alerts the home office needed to respond to during the course of the hack. Situational awareness protocols are used to validate threat assessments either systematically or manually to conclude the veracity of the risk. Cybercriminals understand how to exploit basic human behaviors and regularly test their assumptions through a variety of techniques. More advanced techniques increasingly involve the influence of a user's behavior and perception through the introduction of misinformation. This explains one reason why the attacks are harder to discover and, harder still, to assess the extent of the attack's damage, leading to delays in comprehensive remediation, if achieved at all. A Reuter's article reported that Target did not disclose the security breach until after a security blogger posted reports on his website and journalists called Target to verify the reports. Meanwhile, Neiman Marcus and several other undisclosed retailers experienced similar attack behavior during the same period, allowing hackers to take advantage of the delay in disclosure.

Suggestions for a "Cyberattack Data Clearinghouse" have not yet gained support. "Threat intelligence sharing is ineffective," concluded

a Department of Homeland Security survey reviewed by *Nextgov*.*
Nonetheless, the speed, scale, and asymmetry of attacks in use argue
for a legally protected, early report/response mechanism to share
attack behavior with industry verticals as early warning systems. These
self-regulated groups, organized by industry vertical and cross-vertical
channels, should include law enforcement and security advisers in
ways that leverage leading practice and resources more efficiently.

The Securities and Exchange Commission (SEC) published CF
Disclosure Guidance: Topic No. 2, on Cybersecurity in October
2011, which outlines its expectations for SEC registrants on public
disclosure of a cyberattack, yet more is needed to help coordinate
and facilitate the process of disclosure. Cyberattacks are typically
executed with "bespoke," or custom-designed, malware that is used
once and discarded after disclosure. By the time other firms in the
same industry learn of the attack and implement defenses to prevent similar attacks it is already too late. Situational awareness must
be broader than isolated incidents within a firm if the information
and data needed to evaluate threats are to be acquired in a timely
manner.

Reluctance to report is considered common. Two retailers are
reported to have "waited more than two years to admit that they
were victims in 2007 of notorious hacker Albert Gonzalez, who
was accused of masterminding the theft and reselling of millions
of credit cards and ATM numbers," according to the same Reuters
report in January 2014. The reluctance to make public disclosure
is understandable given the market reaction and subsequent fallout
that ensues.

Target's profit for the holiday shopping period fell 46% from the
same quarter the year before; the number of transactions suffered its
biggest decline since the retailer began reporting the statistic in 2008.
Target also suffered a decline in sales of between 2% and 6% after
disclosure and was the subject of lawsuits and legal costs negotiated
with credit card holders and insurance carriers as a result of the cyberattack. A *New York Times* article quotes one source as saying that the

---

* "A Review of the Department of Homeland Security's Missions and Performance,"
  A Report by Senator Tom Coburn Ranking Member Committee on Homeland
  Security and Governmental Affairs, U.S. Senate, 113th Congress, January 2015.

"total damage to banks and retailers" resulting from the Target network security breach "could exceed \$18 billion."

The externalities of cyber risk are a difficult challenge to resolve but can and should be debated as part of the framework for addressing the long-term costs of cybercrime. The backstory of Target's hack demonstrates how a firm's lack of situational awareness creates self-inflicted damage. It should be noted that several firms suffered from a similar attack but Target's negative press is, in part, a result of the size of the firm and damage caused by the hackers.

Situational awareness is an important component of the cognitive tool kit for cybersecurity professionals. The effectiveness of situational awareness is only as strong as the quality, completeness, and timeliness of the information and data observed in the environment. The weaknesses of situational awareness have been noted by researchers. "The test of Situation Awareness as a construct will be in its ability to be operationalized in terms of objective, clearly specified independent (stimulus manipulation) and dependent (response difference) variables … Otherwise, SA will be yet another buzzword to cloak scientists' ignorance" (Flach, 1995, p. 155). Recognizing the inherent limitations, the lesson from Target should be that situational awareness cannot be taken lightly and must assume a role as part of an integrated program in organizations as an arsenal of tools to limit, deter, and/or prevent damage from an attack.

Researchers have only scratched the surface of the cognitive skills needed to enable asymmetric countermeasures in cybersecurity. One of the risks cited in situational awareness is complacency, "Assuming everything is under control affects vigilance. When things are slow, tasks are routine, and/or when objectives have been achieved, complacency can occur."* This is prudent advice for all risk professionals and especially so for cybersecurity. It is now time to delve into a new field of research called Cognitive Security, Intelligence and Security Informatics (ISI) to see how it can be used to help enhance security measures. ISI involves a set of countermeasures to address cognitive hacking.

"Cognitive informatics is the multidisciplinary study of cognition and information sciences, which investigates human information

---

* https://www.uscg.mil/auxiliary/training/tct/chap5.pdf

processing mechanisms and processes and their engineering applications in computing," according to Pacific Northwest National Laboratory (PNNL). PNNL's research focuses on developing technologies to broaden the integration of human interface with technology to improve learning and decision making, among other benefits. Cognitive informatics is multidisciplinary in approach and is informed by research in psychology, behavioral science, neuroscience, artificial intelligence, and linguistics.

Security professionals are increasingly fighting new battles in cyberattacks against asymmetric weapons. The ease with which hackers continue to penetrate traditional defensive posture calls for a more robust set of measures using smart systems and a better understanding of the vulnerabilities at the intersection of the human–system integration. Training and awareness campaigns are still important but are woefully deficient. Even astute technology professionals are frequently fooled. A recent news account reported that Facebook founder Mark Zuckerberg's social media accounts were hacked.* Zuckerberg's accounts were compromised by a group called OurMine that took credit, claiming Zuckerberg's credentials were discovered in a database of compromised LinkedIn accounts. This story highlights a simple truth about cyber risk that we take for granted. If we choose to actively engage social media, email, and other communications channels, each of us is responsible for our own security. However, when you choose to do so from your workplace you expose the firm to cyberattacks, unwittingly compromising investments in security for the entire firm. The hack of Zuckerberg's social media accounts was an opportunistic and simple one executed to gain exposure for OurMine but should serve as a warning that we too leave a digital trail of data behind.

"Physical and syntactic attacks occur totally within the computing and networking infrastructure, seeking vulnerabilities, without the intervention of human interaction. A cognitive hack requires the *user* to change behavior via the introduction of misinformation that violates the integrity of the overall system."† Cognitive hacks can take many

---

* http://www.usatoday.com/story/tech/news/2016/06/06/mark-zuckerbergs-social
-media-accounts-hacked/85477432/
† http://citeseerx.ist.psu.edu/viewdoc/download?doi=10.1.1.87.6587&rep=rep1&type
=pdf

forms, some of which do not involve an attack on network infrastructure, but may simply include "the provisioning of misinformation, the
intentional distribution or insertion of false or misleading information intended to influence a reader's decisions or activities," according to Dr. Paul Thompson of the Thayer School of Engineering and
Department of Computer Science at Dartmouth College.

Cognitive hacking continues to spread in ways that have yet to be
fully defined. One definition describes it as follows. Cognitive hackers manipulate a user's perception and rely on his or her changed
actions to carry out the attack. Effective countermeasures must aim
at preventing misinformation through authentication, collaborative
filtering, and linguistic analysis. In 1981, Carl Landwehr observed
that "Without a precise definition of what security means and how
a computer can behave, it is meaningless to ask whether a particular
computer system is secure."* Landwehr's point is that we must define
security more precisely to account for the risks we wish to mitigate.
The open nature of the Internet makes it an ideal medium for spreading misinformation. ISI is one example of how computer scientists
are pushing the boundaries of security to advance countermeasures
in cognitive and semantic attacks to build trust back into networked
information systems.†

The concept of cognitive hacking, ISI, as the name implies, is a
cross fertilization of several disciplines currently gaining traction.
Security informatics serves as the core platform for delivery of countermeasures to semantic attacks. Why focus on semantic attacks?
Semantic attacks are characterized as campaigns that use misinformation and deception to successfully evade the defenses of organizations.
The goal of the attacker is to hack the mind of the user cognitively to
influence the user's perception and behavior. Think of a cognitive hack
as one of the methods a hacker uses as a countermeasure to obscure
situational awareness. The obvious result is gaining permission to
enter the organization around its own defenses.

Cognitive hacks are simple, easy to deploy, and most importantly,
effective. For example, if you have ever gotten an unsolicited email
asking you to click on a link to address a problem with an old bankcard

---

* http://www.ists.dartmouth.edu/docs/ch.doc
† http://dl.acm.org/citation.cfm?id=2500948

account you no longer use you may have unknowingly been the victim
of a cognitive hack. Social media has also become a popular source for
hackers who pose as HR recruiters, using links to factious job post-
ings luring the user to set up personal profile accounts only to be used
by hackers to exploit personal information for future attacks.

Schneier describes a semantic attack as "attacks that target how, we
as humans, assign value to content." Schneier considered "the human/
computer interface as the least secure interface on the internet."*
Semantic countermeasures (behavioral algorithms) are also considered ideally suited to address insider threats, an important focus in
security. Semantic attack vectors are more subtle and covert, differing
from brute force attacks that require security professionals to defend
against attacks using intelligence methods to measure trusted sources.

In July 2010, in a real-life example, the Associated Press (AP)
uncovered a semantic hack through a U.S. government-funded effort
to create a Twitter-like social network in Cuba called ZunZuneo. It
was quite a success, shutting down only after it became too big, too
fast. The humanitarian agency behind the project—United States
Agency for International Development (USAID)—said, "It just
wanted to create a network where users could talk among themselves."
The Associated Press article was picked up broadly, including in the
Washington Post, and caused a row in political circles upon its disclosure. The optics of the details disclosed by the AP article prompted
a public response by USAID, the governmental development agency
that created the website.

USAID posted a statement on its website, dated Thursday, April 2,
2014. In reference to the AP article on "Cuban Twitter" on April 3,
2014, USAID spokesperson Matt Herrick issued the following
statement:

> It is longstanding U.S. policy to help Cubans increase the ability to
> communicate with each other and with the outside world. Working
> with resources provided by Congress for exactly this purpose. USAID
> is proud of its work in Cuba to provide basic humanitarian assistance,
> promote human rights and universal freedoms, and to help informa-
> tion flow more freely to the Cuban people. All of our work in Cuba,

---

* http://www.counterpane.com/crypto-gram-0010.html

including this project, was reviewed in detail in 2013 by the Government Accountability Office and found to be consistent with U.S. law and appropriate under oversight controls.

It is also no secret that in hostile environments, governments take steps to protect the partners we are working with on the ground. The purpose of the ZunZuneo was to create a platform for Cubans to speak freely among themselves, period. At the initial stages, the grantee sent tech news, sports scores, weather, and trivia to build interest and engage Cubans. After that, Cubans were able to talk among themselves, and we are proud of that. USAID is a development agency and we work all over the world to help people exercise their universal rights and freedoms.*

Cognitive hacks have been around for some time but the sophistication of the attack has grown. In August 2000, a press release became widely circulated in major media news sources reporting that Emulex, a server and storage provider, had revised earnings from a $0.25 per share gain to a $0.15 loss and lowered net earnings from the previous quarter. Emulex shares plummeted more than 50% within minutes of the release, from $104 to $43 per share. The story was totally fabricated by a 23-year-old hacker named Mark Jacob who had previously lost $100,000 in a short sale trade. The hack was an attempt to recover his losses, which he did fourfold, until his indictment for securities fraud. Jacob was able to achieve his hack outside of the domain of a computer network through the use of manipulation and deception to change the perception of investors. "The internet's open environment makes it ideal for hackers to launch a variety of semantic attacks."†

Semantic attacks are defined as the execution of the delivery of misinformation through the use of various media, including the Internet, to create the impression of a trusted source for the sole purpose of changing behavior. The real difference in semantic attacks, as opposed to other forms of cyberattacks, is that the user is the target of the attack, in contrast to the network (physical attack) or operating logic (syntactic attack) of the hardware. The Cuban ZunZuneo and the Mark Jacob stock scheme are examples of semantic attacks.

* https://www.washingtonpost.com/lifestyle/style/usaid-effort-to-undermine-cuban-government-with-fake-twitter-another-anti-castro-failure/2014/04/03/c0142cc0-bb75-11e3-9a05-c739f29ccb08_story.html
† http://www.ists.dartmouth.edu/library/300.pdf

Many people recognize "phishing" as one of the most common types of semantic attacks but it's clearly not the only one. A newer version of semantic attacks has begun to emerge called "malvertisement." A malvertisement is an online advertisement that is infected with a virus or malicious computer code, which takes advantage of placement of online advertising to steadily disperse malware to new users. Semantic attacks have proven very effective in the past; however, as Internet users have become more aware of these tricks hackers continue to evolve.

Cyberattacks aimed at organizations have increased since 2009, with 91% of all organizations hit by cyberattacks in 2013.* The vast majority of organizations rely heavily on email for internal and external communication. Thus, email has become a very attractive platform from which to initiate cyberattacks against organizations. Attackers often use social engineering to encourage recipients to press a link or open a malicious webpage or attachment. According to Trend Micro, attacks, particularly those against government agencies and large corporations, are largely dependent on spear-phishing emails.

Social media, popular video websites, and church and dating websites have increasingly become platforms used by cybercriminals to execute malware. The goal remains the same for hackers but the tactics are less transparent to web surfers. It is easy to see that the diversity of cognitive and semantic hacks requires an entirely new set of tools and why a defensive strategy is ineffective in preventing, correcting, or detecting cognitive hacks. The good news is that promising early stage defensive and offensive strategies are being developed to deal with cognitive hacking.

In response to the rise of semantic hacks, a community has emerged from a very diverse set of disciplines to explore scientific approaches to cybersecurity. Collectively, a new science is evolving called Cognitive Security (CogSec). Consider cognitive security a tree with many branches, each focused on solving security at the human–machine intersection. There is growing recognition that cybersecurity requires advanced approaches, similar to the ones used by hackers, to counter the sophistication of this elusive adversary. One of the largest and most active branches of CogSec is found in the research on ISI.

---

* http://www.humanipo.com/news/37983/91-of-organisations-hit-by-cyber

New research in ISI is advancing rapidly into a cross-disciplinary field of study focused on human interactions in cyberspace. ISI is an interdisciplinary approach that includes research topics in information technologies, computer science, public policy, bioinformatics, and social and behavior science, and involves academic researchers as well as local, state, and federal law enforcement and intelligence experts and other intelligence agencies in support of counterterrorism and homeland security missions geared toward prevention, preparedness, and response to terrorist acts.

Since 2005, the ISI research community has been advancing an impressive array of research results that are both technically innovative and practically relevant. ISI uses computational approaches to automate the extraction of causal knowledge and social behavior of, say, a terrorist organization from online textual data. The types of causal knowledge and social behavior include actions, preconditions and effects, and action hierarchy. Examples include the monitoring and evaluation of social media and other online conversations between terrorist and other bad actors to understand changes in group behavior to assess threats associated with terrorist groups and within the hacker community.

ISI is closely associated with law enforcement and military cyber defensive strategies, but that is beginning to change. Similar methods are developing in parallel in the private sector and increasingly being used in vendor platforms as advanced security counter-defense measures. Private security vendors are also developing new tools to address threats, such as insider threat and deception detection software using behavioral algorithms. Demand for more effective security will continue to grow as more advanced and persistent threats rise sharply. Manual processes are less effective against a high volume of asymmetric attacks used today. Researchers are also exploring a variety of security methods in recognition of the challenge of developing effective machine learning systems.

Let's stop for a moment to understand better the topic of machine learning. The term "machine learning" is often tossed around very loosely in the marketing of vendor cybersecurity services with as much hype and mystery as "big data." So let's be very clear about the current state of machine learning and its limits today to gauge the benefits of further research to come. Machine learning is real and is being used successfully in certain applications such as Google's driverless cars, to predict fraud, detect terrorist activity, and recommend products to customers. Machine learning requires technology applied to huge quantities of data and interdisciplinary expertise in statistics, data mining, machine learning, artificial intelligence, cybersecurity, and more.

There are four types of machine learning algorithms organized around a taxonomy used to produce a desired outcome for each type: (1) supervised learning; (2) unsupervised learning; (3) semisupervised learning; and (4) reinforcement learning. "Supervised learning is the most common type used by 70 percent of algorithms," according to Wayne Thompson, manager of data science technologies at SAS. Supervised learning is "trained" using examples where the desired outcome is known. Unsupervised learning is used in approximately 10% to 20% of machine learning algorithms. The algorithms are not "trained" to find the right answer but instead must find the hidden patterns or structure in data. Semisupervised learning is a hybrid approach using both supervised learning and unsupervised learning techniques to "train" algorithms using a ratio of each approach. Finally, with reinforcement learning the algorithm discovers for itself which actions yield the greatest rewards through trial and error. Reinforcement algorithms require three components: the agent—the learner or decision maker; the environment—everything the agent interacts with; and actions—what the agent can do with the data.

Regardless of the methods used, the algorithm requires an iterative cycle of trial and error to develop predictive models over time. Adjustments are made by data scientists to find the right fit of parameters to gain confidence in the model's predictive capabilities. A small number of large firms are using big data for cybersecurity. According to a 2014 Microsoft survey of security executives, only 16% of sample firms have active programs in place and are in early stage development. Respondents in the survey plan to focus on user activity (insider threat), external threats, network traffic, policy violations, endpoints, and application behavior. Microsoft's survey does not address how the respondents determined their priority ranking of areas of focus nor explain whether their assumptions changed after conducting an analysis of data. The Ponemon Institute facilitated the survey.

One clear implied outcome from the Microsoft survey and SAS's modeling exercise in cyber analytics is the need for analytical skills in IT security to build these programs in-house. The math is complicated and is still developing as researchers learn how to transfer success from other disciplines to cybersecurity. Firms that use vendors to design and build their programs will be dependent on consultants until a new discipline is created in-house. The costs and time needed to build these skills are available to the largest firms but how will smaller, less financially capable firms fare in the race to cognitive security? There is more good news on that front as well. Cyber education is growing and funded in partnership with grants by government, private, and public capital and institutions of higher education. In time, a new cadre of cybersecurity experts will contribute to new advances in security.

"The IEEE International Conference (ISI) on Intelligence and Security Informatics has evolved from its traditional orientation of intelligence and security domain towards a more integrated alignment of multiple domains, including technology, human cognition, organizations, and security. The scientific community has increasingly recognized the need to address intelligence and security threats by understanding the interrelationships between these different components, and by integrating recent advances from different domains," according to the IEEE website.*

Four main verticals have emerged as key disciplines in ISI: Data Science and Analytics in Security Informatics; Security Infrastructure and Tools; Human Behavior in the Security Applications; and Organizational, National, and International Issues in Counter-terrorism or Security Protection. IEEE has prioritized research submissions across each of these disciplines to focus resources and thought leadership.

IEEE is the self-described "world's largest technical professional organization dedicated to advancing technology for the benefit of humanity."† The organization promotes research publications and standards in cybersecurity, conducts conferences and educational events, and has a global membership and focus. However, as you can

---

* http://isi2015.wixsite.com/isi-2015
† https://duckduckgo.com/?q=cybersecurity+associations&t=ffab

imagine, a growing number of cybersecurity course providers have exploded onto the scene with constituent groups ranging from educators, Homeland Security, space, military, industry, telecommunications, trade associations, and many more.

Cybersecurity talent is in high demand, with higher education, nonprofit and for-profit organizations experiencing a surge in new entrants into the field. As the number of professional and corporate trained cyber hackers and security professionals grow in the coming decades, the need for a more advanced cyber governance and risk management framework is needed to account for cyber ethics and cyber law in a world with people who possess the skills to hack into any system.*

The Association for the Advancement of Artificial Intelligence, in cooperation with Stanford University, has sponsored a series of symposiums in computer research bringing alive the vision of exploring the interaction between humans and machines. The most recent series put forth seven symposia on Artificial Intelligence (AI) and the Mitigation of Human Error, Multiagent Learning, Social Intelligent Human–Robot Interactions, Intelligent Systems for Team Work, Ethical & Moral Considerations in Non-Human Agents, Studies in Social Media and Human-Generated Content, and Well-Being Computing. Previous series have been equally diverse, with topics such as "Social Hacking and Cognitive Security on the Internet and New Media" and "the Intersection of Robust Intelligence and Trust in Autonomous Systems." Large tech firms have already begun branding their cognitive security offerings along with private equity joining the fray with rounds of acquisitions in anticipation of high adoption rates in the near future. Cognitive security is being touted beyond cybersecurity, with some vendors making the case for its use in managing energy; however, I suspect this will expand rapidly to enterprise risk, integrating compliance, risk, audit, IT security, and more.

Security professionals need to develop new processes in preparation for the emerging cognitive security environment being developed. The building blocks that lead to a cognitive risk program include considerations on three dimensions: *data management and analysis*, *technology redesign*, and *cognitive risk* at the *human–machine interaction*. The final

---

* https://duckduckgo.com/?q=university+associated+cyber+security+initiatives&t=ffab

chapter will go into some detail for developing a "bridge" from today's defensive strategy of hardening the enterprise to an active cognitive risk framework. The first step in the transition to a new environment starts with a conversation about risk. Although this may sound intuitive, conversations about risk and uncertainty are more complex than most believe.

The topic of risk is made more complex by counterintuitive factors we each take for granted. The first of these factors is language. Earlier I mentioned the conversation between Apple and the director of the FBI. Each side framed the risk, access to meta-intelligence, differently without reconciling outcomes to expectations on both sides. Conflicting views of risk are a natural result of unresolved differences in how each side views a risk, leading to distrust. The language of risk is a major reason organizations develop "blind spots" to certain risks, resulting in a failure to move their risk program forward. These blind spots are avoidable but predictable, as displayed in the public debate about the iPhone®.

Heuristics are the shortcuts we use to solve complex problems when simple answers are not available. Heuristics and intuition may lead to errors in judgment because the processes are often unconscious, leading to a failure to see the mistakes we make in our analysis. Behavioral and cognitive science makes us more aware of these unconscious failings, allowing security and risk professionals to recognize the pitfalls and make corrective adjustments before communications deteriorate.

By understanding the role of human behavior and leveraging behavioral science findings, the designers, developers, and engineers of information infrastructure can address real and perceived obstacles to productivity and provide more effective security (Predd et al., 2008; Pfleeger et al., 2010). There is growing evidence to suggest the importance of including some element of human behavior into security systems, but what does that mean exactly? Initial studies have focused on several areas of interest, including how trust is established on the web, changes in employee compliance (Lerner and Tiedens, 2006), the effect of emotional stressors (Klein and Salas, 2001), and other effects outside of the norms of behavior.

A balance has yet to be struck between traditional security measures and behavioral concepts. The aforementioned studies point to a focus on internal behavior, specifically targeted at the insider threat. Several authors have suggested that the insider represents the largest threat actor; however, this metric should be taken with a grain of salt. The focus on internal threats that are now easier to recall because of Edward Snowden leaves firms exposed to even greater risk. Availability bias is the belief that easy to find data or the frequency of recent data validates the proof of a belief. Edward Snowden has become the main threat in cybersecurity without quantifiable data to prove this is a universal risk. Snowden is a tail risk: huge impact, low probability risk. Let's call this the "Edward Snowden" effect, after the former CIA employee and National Security Agency contractor who disclosed the government's global surveillance program. This is not to say that insiders do not represent a threat; the question is whether it should be considered the highest risk. Insiders' access to customer and business data represents a risk that is more easily identifiable and preventable with routine internal controls and surveillance. The cyber threat, on the other hand, is by definition a higher risk given the lack of foreknowledge of the vulnerability or the means by which the attacker is able to steal data.

The risk of confirmation bias from high-profile events may lead to a narrowing of focus on known threats at the expense of missing the circumstances leading up to new vulnerabilities in the future. Libicki and Pfleeger (2004) have documented the difficulties in "collecting the dots" before an analyst can take the next step to connect them. If a "dot" is not as visible as it should be, it can be overlooked or given insufficient attention during subsequent analysis.

One such "dot" is the entry of millennials into the workforce. As the workforce of the future changes from baby boomers to millennials, the risk of semantic attacks is becoming more acute. Millennials are more adept at engaging in a variety of social media sites from work and through mobile devices, exposing themselves and their employers to cyber hacking. With the proliferation of social "news" outlets for content and the perceived safety of sharing personal data online by millennials, social media has become an easy target in cyberattacks. As mentioned previously, Mark Zuckerberg, an uber millennial who is tech savvy, had his social media account hacked using an old password from LinkedIn, another social media platform. Millennials are more likely to trust these online services, having known few other alternatives, making this generation more susceptible to cyber risks in the future.

Millennials have adopted entirely different trust models than their baby boom predecessors who spent less time searching the web for their news and entertainment. The millennial generation, broadly defined as this generation's early teens to mid-30s adults, represent roughly 25% of the U.S. population and are the first generation of Americans born in the mobile digital age. Websites such as Facebook and Google are perceived by millennials as the utility of their day. Mobile apps, media, and other digital content is taken for granted given 1 billion+ people globally use these platforms. Millennials take security for granted as well, but should they?

As technology converts old industry to new eCommerce platforms ranging from how we pay for products and services to ordering custom-made clothing and more, we expose ourselves without the assurance of trust on the Internet. Interestingly, organizations have evidence of the threats of social media yet are reluctant to prevent access and instead have expanded vulnerability with the issuance of mobile phones and other communication devices, leaving firms more exposed. These too are the contradictions in cybersecurity. Simple measures can be taken without huge expense but the "blind spots" persist.

Trust must be redefined as technology accelerates at an unprecedented speed. Big tech firms, in collaboration with industry leaders, are developing entirely new customer interface platforms using robots with AI, machine learning, and voice response systems that learn from interactions on the web, changing our perception of trust. Mark Zuckerberg's Facebook is one of the first big tech firms to deploy chatbots for business users on a large scale. "Facebook boasts more than one billion messages are sent between businesses and users via Messenger," according to an April 2016 *Fortune* article.* Several technology developers are experimenting with chatbot personalities, including Microsoft's now infamous "Tay," who learned how to become a racist from Twitter users. Microsoft's experience with Tay should teach us very valuable lessons about the need for safeguards when using AI in the public domain and points to the inherent limitations that still exist.

---

* http://fortune.com/2016/04/12/facebook-chat-bots-messenger-app/

A user's ability to discern trust accurately is complicated by the diversity of user-generated content and a plethora of disruptive entrants in the marketplace of ideas for media and digital content. As traditional news outlets of trusted content increasingly transition to today's 24/7 digital content, the line of trust on the web will blur further. In my opinion, today's social media dominated content is much less trustworthy, exposing users and organizations to higher risk and may help to explain, in part, the accelerated growth of cyberattacks. As user adoption of new technology grows, we are exposed to more opportunities for an attack without our knowledge.

According to a 2014 Symantec Internet Security Threat Report, "the primary motive behind social networking attacks is monetary gain." The report outlines that phishing attacks are evolving, "moving further away from email and into the social media landscape." Nonetheless, the same techniques that security professionals have observed in phishing and spam emails are being leveraged in social media campaigns.* Cognitive hacks are disguised as "fake offers," "fake Like buttons or Likejacking," "fake plugins or Internet extensions," and "fake apps." Given this trend, the definition of security must be reexamined to combat diminished trust at the human–machine interaction. Stakeholders, from content and solution providers to security analysts, must evaluate how to restore trust on the Internet. A concerted effort is needed by all parties to narrow the corridor of risk against a persistent and growing community of sophisticated adversaries.

How does a corporate security analyst assess the trustworthiness of content among a universe of social media sites via a mobile "bring your own device" (BYOD) environment? Social media is a global phenomenon that blurs the lines of trust in personal and business relationships. In a December 2014 report by Cylance, an endpoint security firm investigated an Iranian base of attackers operating undetected for at least two years before discovery. "The attackers, dubbed "Threat Group-2889" or "TG-2889," appeared to be Iranian-sponsored hackers whose activities were documented by the security company in a December 2014 report investigating a campaign called "Operation

---

* http://www.securityweek.com/next-big-cybercrime-vector-social-media

Cleaver."* The attackers set up at least 25 fake LinkedIn accounts, creating personas, photographs, and information from well-known corporations in the United States, South Korea, and Kuwait, among other countries.

"Perhaps the most chilling evidence collected in this campaign was the targeting and compromise of transportation networks and systems such as airlines and airports in South Korea, Saudi Arabia and Pakistan," according to the Cylance report. "The level of access seemed ubiquitous: Active Directory domains were fully compromised, along with entire Cisco Edge switches, routers, and internal networking infrastructure. Fully compromised VPN credentials meant their entire remote access infrastructure and supply chain was under the control of the Cleaver team, allowing permanent persistence under compromised credentials. They achieved complete access to airport gates and their security control systems, potentially allowing them to spoof gate credentials. They gained access to PayPal and Go Daddy credentials, allowing them to make fraudulent purchases and allowed unfettered access to the victim's domains."

The group behind Operation Cleaver had been active (on LinkedIn) since at least 2012, targeting more than 50 companies across 16 countries, including organizations in the military, government, oil and gas, energy and utilities, chemical, transportation, healthcare, education, telecommunications, technology, aerospace, and defense sectors. The remaining fake accounts were set up as supporting personas to give the key players credibility and believability within the site. The hackers posed as executive recruiters to approach members on the site and may have used spear phishing and malicious web links to increase their success rate.

This attack was not the first of its kind. "In May 2014, cyber intelligence company iSIGHT Partners analyzed a campaign in which attackers had used over a dozen fake personas on various social networking websites."† It is shocking to believe that such a massive attack was achieved so simply using syntactic and semantic methods.

---

* http://www.securityweek.com/iranian-sponsored-hackers-hit-critical-infrastructure
  -companies-research
† http://www.securityweek.com/iranian-hackers-targeted-us-officials-elaborate-social
  -media-attack-operation

"Simplicity of approach" and "simplicity of execution" are recurring themes in each of the major attacks we have reviewed. Simplicity is used to gain trust, obscuring the intent of hackers and allowing them to trick users into changing their behavior.

Researchers have also formulated general themes about the interaction of cybersecurity and cognitive risks. The first theme, as we have discussed, is improving human–machine interactions using technology to determine the trustworthiness of the interaction. Second, security analysts, overloaded by the sheer volume of threats large and small, suffer from *cognitive load*, leading to a diminished ability to process all of the threats efficiently with the appropriate level of prioritization. Researchers are exploring new approaches to augment the highest priority threats needing the attention of security professionals (Miller, 1956; Chase and Simon, 1973; Mack and Rock, 1998; Burke, 2010).

Simons and Chabris (1999) and Simons and Jensen (2009) later identified the effects of cognitive load more succinctly as *inattentional blindness*, referring to a person's inability to notice unexpected events when concentrating on a primary task. Third, researchers noted significant cognitive bias in security professionals resulting in vast differences in how one analyst perceives a threat versus others. Each threat can be experienced differently when factors such as aptitude, training, or inability are taken into account. These factors are called heuristics, a main cause of misconception in the judgment of risk. Humans develop expertise and gain experience by knowing what to do when faced with similar experiences. When the experience is out of the ordinary these same skills tend to fail us simply because we have not prepared nor have the skills to adjust. This is not a personal failure; it is a natural result of ineptness. This is why we need to improve the language of risk. Ineptness is most often used in a negative connotation when someone fails to recognize what others see as obvious, often after the fact. Ineptness is a signal that either additional training is needed or a different set of tools is required to address uncommon risks. And, lastly, lacking a quantitative approach to threat assessment, security analysts are unable to measure risks uniformly, settling on qualitative measures of likelihood and impact that are inherently inaccurate, producing wide variance in over- and underestimations of risks.

Hold on! If technology is not enough and humans can't be trusted, how do we build intuitive situational awareness in cyber defense? The Apple ecosystem is a good proxy for system engineering design. Simplicity, intuitive integration and functionality allowed Steve Jobs to reinvent the mobile phone into a smartphone. Cybersecurity requires additional elements but the concepts are applicable. Layered security technology must be redesigned into smart cybersecurity.

The genius of Steve Jobs is in how he transformed function into simple utility. The smartphone's form changed incrementally but its utility is remarkable. Jobs was fanatical about details; he instinctively understood how cognition operates on two levels: intuition (heuristics and biases) and analytical concepts that require more time and energy. The more time, energy, and mental resources needed to solve a problem the less likely the outcomes are uniform. Jobs reimagined the smartphone to make it simple and intuitive. A small child can pick up an iPhone and begin to use it. BlackBerry, on the other hand, struggles to compete with the iPhone's simplicity. If we want humans to do a better job at cybersecurity we have only two options. First, make security simple and intuitive for the human mind or use computer technology to correct and avoid errors in human judgment. Let's address the second problem first and return to the first problem near the end of this chapter.

Having already introduced cognitive security, let's return to this topic to look more deeply into the areas associated with human limitations in managing cognitive hacks. Computer scientists and researchers are producing impressive results in the field of AI as a proxy for how technology will be used to simplify security by integrating machine learning and cyber defense capability.

AI solves a number of disparate problems and creates new challenges as well. According to Google researchers, the process for creating machine learning and AI is labor intensive: "we gather large volumes of direct or indirect evidence of relationships of interest, and we apply learning algorithms to generalize from that evidence to new cases of interest. Machine Learning at Google raises deep scientific and engineering challenges. Contrary to much of current theory and practice, the statistics of the data we observe shifts very rapidly, the features of interest change as well, and the volume of data often precludes the use of standard single-machine training algorithms. When learning systems are placed at the core of interactive services in a rapidly changing and sometimes adversarial environment, statistical models need to be combined with ideas from control and game theory, for example when using learning in auction algorithms."*

What is AI and how does it work? AI falls into two or three camps depending on your definition. *Strong AI* (sometimes called General AI) aims to duplicate human intellect: to understand, perceive, have beliefs, and exhibit other cognitive traits normally ascribed to human beings. Strong AI has not been achieved and many believe it is not necessary as long as certain tasks can be performed to get work done. However, there is a great deal of research and controversy surrounding the topic of replicating human intelligence. Suffice it to say, Strong AI is not used for cybersecurity. The second form of AI is called *Weak AI*. IBM's Deep Blue, known for beating chess masters, is a form of Weak AI, which is at most a simulation of a cognitive process but is not itself a cognitive process. The third version is a hybrid of the two called *Narrow AI*, a branch of Weak AI with subsets of sophistication from the very simple (Apple's Siri®) to more complex learning algorithms. In fact, hackers are using Narrow AI in remotely controlled botnets to execute a variety of attack strategies very successfully. Google has demonstrated how "deep learning" systems function by learning layers of representations for tasks such as image and speech recognition. According to Google researchers, "reinforcement learning algorithms can learn to map which actions lead to the best outcomes, they are 'model-free,' meaning the system knows nothing about its world."† Google's DeepMind team designed AlphaGo, described as an intuitive system that beat the European Go Champion and elite player Fan Hui. AlphaGo was taught how to play Go by feeding its neural networks with 30 million Go games played by experts. Go, an abstract strategy board game invented in China 2,500 years ago, is considered to be the most complex board game, with 200 moves per turn versus 20 in chess and more iterations of play than the observable atoms in the universe.

---

* http://research.google.com/pubs/ArtificialIntelligenceandMachineLearning.html
† https://www.technologyreview.com/s/601139/how-google-plans-to-solve
  -artificial-intelligence/

Dr. Simon Stringer, director of the Oxford Centre for Theoretical Neuroscience and Artificial Intelligence, said that "AlphaGo and other deep learning systems are good at specific tasks—be that spotting objects or animals in photos or mastering a game. But these systems work very differently from the human brain and shouldn't be viewed as representing progress towards developing a general, human-like intelligence—which he believes requires an approach guided by biology."*

Deep learning is expected to hold the most promise for a wide range of business applications. In fact, there has been explosive growth in the number of software vendors touting their version of "AI or machine learning" capability, ranging from small entrepreneurs to the largest tech firms. The state of art in AI and machine learning will advance and each improvement must be understood by security professionals to determine the appropriate application of these tools in their cybersecurity practice. The science is advancing rapidly but is not mature enough to apply broadly without a considerable amount of legwork still needed to effectively combat cybercrime. One of the areas where intelligent, autonomous agents have shown a great deal of promise in cyberspace is in the area of deception detection.

Early versions of deception detection have focused on building trust relationships through a history of interactions. More recent research is concerned with applying models of cognitive and behavioral science to a group of intelligent agents, testing the correlation of deception and detection separately among the test group to determine whether intelligent agents can distinguish deception among its members.

Researchers have moved from the lab to real-world applications in deception detection AI capability. A team from MIT claims to have built an AI system that can detect 85% of cyberattacks with high accuracy.† "The new system does not just rely on the artificial intelligence (AI), but also on human input, which researchers call Analyst Intuition (AI), which is why it has been given the name of *Artificial Intelligence Squared* or *AI²*." AI is used to scan more than 3.6 billion lines of log files and presents its findings to an analyst each day. The analyst reviews the data and then identifies which events are positive

---

* http://www.techrepublic.com/article/how-googles-ai-breakthroughs-are-putting
  -us-on-a-path-to-narrow-ai/
† http://thehackernews.com/2016/04/artificial-intelligence-cyber-security.html

for cyberattacks and discards the false-positive events that serve as learning for the AI system on each iteration. The researchers claim higher accuracy in cyber threat detection with each cycle of learning.

AI comprises a diverse subfield of research and practical applications, many so pervasive that observers no longer consider its use AI. To date, simple examples of learning have proven far easier to simulate using computers than the complex nature of human learning. Teaching machines to become expert in more than one area requires a quantum leap in speed, access to data, and algorithms for continuous learning. However, a great deal of progress has been made toward solving these problems. Wide use of intelligent decision support is still a distant goal, albeit the gap is closing rapidly.

Enn Tyugu, a researcher with Cooperative Cyber Defense Center of Excellence, wrote a brief review of potential AI application capability for use in cyber defense. Tyugu zeroed in on the need and challenges of operationalizing AI for cyber defense. "The applications are grouped in categories such as, neural networks, expert systems, search, machine learning, data mining and constraint solving."*

Why is this important? The defensive posture of security professionals will only become more daunting as cybercriminals begin to implement their own form of AI algorithms more broadly.

"The main task facing artificial intelligence [AI] researchers at present is to create an autonomous, AI device fully capable of learning, making informed decisions and modifying its own behavioral patterns in response to external stimuli. It is possible to build highly specialized bespoke systems; it is also possible to build more universal and complex AI, however, such systems are always based upon the limited experience and knowledge of humans in the form of behavioral examples, rules or algorithms."† Inevitably, domain-specific solutions will be linked together to create networks of knowledge that begin to operate in an autonomous fashion.

Why is it so difficult to create autonomous AI? "In order to perform work, AI currently requires algorithms that have been predetermined

---

* https://ccdcoe.org/publications/2011proceedings/ArtificialIntelligenceInCyber
  Defense-Tyugu.pdf
† https://securelist.com/analysis/publications/36325/cyber-expert-artificial-intelligence
  -in-the-realms-of-it-security/

by humans. Nevertheless, attempts to reach the holy grail of true AI are constantly being made and some of them are showing signs of success."* The idea of autonomous weapons in cyberspace has a great deal of appeal; however, there are an equal number of distractors who worry that rapid development of technology in what is called the "Big Four" pose great risks as well. What are the Big Four? Pervasive Computing, Big Data Analytics, Artificial Intelligence, and Cyber Hostility define what one author called the "Four Horsemen of Datapocolypse."†

Why such a dire view of the future in cyberspace? Pervasive computing is descriptive of a concept in which computing is embedded in our work, our play and entertainment, and social interactions. Think of social media sites and the wealth of personal and business data freely surrendered to everyone from around the world as an example. One can easily imagine a world where the integration of social media, entertainment, and business interactions will become indistinguishable. The Internet of Things (IoT) is but one promised version of this virtual world of connectedness. We are creating an artificial world that now rivals the real world in the infrastructure we rely on, services we purchase, and relationships we nurture in virtual networks. Pandora's box has been opened and we can no longer go back and reverse course. Our personal data are now exposed in ways most people have little knowledge of or understanding.

The fear is that attacks can be initiated from anywhere in the world by unknown assailants with increasingly more sophisticated tools. The hack on the CIA chief's email account in October 2015 demonstrates that governments are not in a position to protect us from threats on the web. Internet users are responsible for their own safety when surfing the web and that requires more than education and an understanding of new technologies. Going forward, humans need intelligent agents working behind the scenes helping to defend us in cyberspace because we cannot do so alone. The challenges are not insurmountable and will be overcome in time. What may be more challenging is the development of a framework for humans to engage

---

* https://securelist.com/analysis/publications/36325/cyber-expert-artificial
  -intelligence-in-the-realms-of-it-security/
† http://artificialtimes.com/blog/why-should-we-care-part-1/

in the management of autonomous systems through good governance and legal considerations. The imagination does not have to wonder far to envision how government officials, business leaders, and others could manipulate these tools.

What are the exposures? Social media presents a treasure trove of data about what we like, what we buy, how we spend our time, and a host of other information that can be used for surveillance of citizens with the use of big data analytics. However, the deep web, represented by data stored behind firewalls, in networks and storage devices used by government, medical, business, and personal users increasingly is exposed to attack. Internet users currently, wittingly or unwittingly, accept these risks given the small percentage of victims actually experiencing known breaches of security. As these numbers continue to grow, expectations for more elaborate security will be demanded. Trends in ransomware serve as one example of disturbing new trends in cyber theft used by hackers.

Ransomware is the latest example of sophisticated malware used by cybercriminals. It targets police departments, banks, hospitals, and mobile phones, encrypting parts of a computer, device, or an entire business network until users pay using Bitcoin in the hope, but not guarantee, of freeing their data from the criminal. In some cases a small ransom is paid, as was the case with a police department in Tewksbury, Massachusetts; others have paid higher amounts. Disturbingly, security professionals and the FBI have recommended negotiating with criminals and setting up a budget for the practice. More proactive methods are needed to defend against this growing threat. Seventy-four percent of security professionals in a 2014 ThreatTrack survey of 250 analysts responded they had been the target of cyber extortion and many have given up and paid a ransom to free their data. Ransom amounts have been small enough that the inconvenience and cost of system remediation have proven to be a successful business endeavor for entrepreneurial hackers. Flashpoint, an intelligence research firm, followed one Russian hacker's ransomware campaign and estimated his or her annual income was $90,000 per year. The hacker employed a small team of surrogates who presumably deployed botnets in a ring of ransomware theft.*

---

* https://www.helpnetsecurity.com/2016/06/02/ransomware-boss-earns-90000/

Ransomware attacks are growing. Security researchers from Kaspersky Labs reported a Trojan program, Svpeng, used on Russia's three largest banks was initiated from Google Play to collect users' data. "When instructed by its server, the malware attempted to block the user's phone and displayed a message demanding payment of a US$500 'fee' for alleged criminal activity."* That ransomware function was further improved and a new variant of Svpeng was identified on mobile phones outside of Russia. Ninety-one percent of users affected by the new version were based in the United States, but the malware also infected devices in the United Kingdom, Switzerland, Germany, India, and Russia, noted a Kaspersky risk analyst.

JP Morgan promised to double spending for risk management and security from $250 million to $500 million. Half a billion dollars is a tidy sum that will inevitably grow if better alternatives are not developed. The "cyber paradox" is exemplified as the endless cycle of massive spending on cybersecurity with no evidence of risk reduction in security. Going forward, the question of how to solve the cyber paradox remains. Will an integration of offensive and defensive security measures using some form of AI and machine learning make a difference? Clearly we can no longer continue to take incremental approaches in response to each cyberattack. But each time the stakes are raised hackers respond with even more sophisticated workarounds. Cyberwarfare has an analogy in conventional war, with each side seeking advantage through intelligence gathering on tactics and strategy. Defensive technologies, such as encryption, created to protect our data have become weapons used to hold business and individuals hostage. It is also clear that cyber skills are fungible; as new technology and techniques become known in the public domain hackers are as likely to adopt them as are security professionals. In response, security professionals need intelligence gathering to inform not only their response but also any adjustments required under certain threat conditions. Equally important is the need for security providers to consider how their products and services might be used or modified by those with the intent to harm others.

---

* http://www.pcworld.com/article/2362980/russian-mobile-banking-trojan-gets-ransomware-features-starts-targeting-us-users.html

The cyber paradox is also confounded by the lack of a sense of urgency by the general public to the threats of cybercrime. Warnings and training programs on the risk of cyber threats have proven ineffective, baffling law enforcement and security professionals alike. I have coined this phenomenon "risk deafness" to explain why this happens, supported by research. Education and awareness alone have many drawbacks and have proven to be ineffective tools in cyber risk and risk management more broadly. Risk deafness is partly caused by poor articulation in the language of risk compounded by cognitive overload created by the expectation of individuals to grasp and perfectly execute hundreds of internal policies and procedures. This topic and the research are reviewed in more detail later but these themes are relevant as justification for developing intelligent systems to support security professionals' efforts to build trust in networked information systems.

"With estimates that at least 95 percent of email traffic in the world consists of spam and phishing, it's obvious another solution is necessary," according to Marcus Rogers, director of Purdue's Cyber Forensics Lab. "Artificial intelligence is among the next steps being considered, combining technology and the human ability to look at information quickly and make a decision."* Around the same time of the Svpeng attack reported by Kaspersky, an improved version of malware was used to attack Bank of America and other large banks, called Dyre. This variant "found a way to bypass Web encryption, known as secure sockets layer (SSL)."† Reports of Dyre's use to attack cloud and file-sharing service providers such as Salesforce. com, Dropbox, and Chubby were not verified for purposes of this book; however, if found to be true the implications for AI are obvious. Where does the digital footprint of cybercrime take us from here?

---

* https://polytechnic.purdue.edu/profile/rogersmk
† http://arstechnica.com/security/2014/09/dyre-malware-branches-out-from-banking
  -adds-corporate-espionage/

References

Burke, L. M., Fueling strategies to optimize performance: Training high or training low? *Scandinavian Journal of Medicine & Science in Sports*, 20. Blackwell Publishing Ltd, 1600-0838.

Chase, W. G. and Simon, H. A., "Perception in chess," *Cognitive Psychology*, 4, 1973, 55–81.

Endsley, M. R., Design and evaluation for situation awareness enhancement. *In Proceedings of the Human Factors Society 32 Annual Meeting* (pp. 97–101). Santa Monica, CA: Human Factors and Ergonomic Society, 1988a.

Endsley, M. R., Situation Awareness Global Assessment Technique (SAGAT). *In Proceedings of the National Aerospace and Electronics Conference* (pp. 789–795). New York: IEEE, 1988b.

Flach, J. M., "Situation Awareness: Proceed with Caution," *Human Factors* 37(1), 1995, 149–157.

Goldberg, J. and von Nitzsch, R., Behavioral Finance. Chichester: Wiley. First published in German under the title Behavioral Finance by FinanzBuch Verlag GmbH. Translated from German by Adriana Morris, 2001.

Kahneman, D. and Tversky, A. (Eds.), *Choices, Values, and Frames*, Cambridge University Press, 2000.

Klein, G. A. and Salas, E. (Eds.), *Linking Expertise and Naturalistic Decision Making*, Erlbaum, 2001.

Lerner, J. S. and Tiedens, L. Z., "Portrait of the Angry Decision Maker: How Appraisal Tendencies Shape Anger's Influence on Cognition," *Journal of Behavioral Decision Making (Special Issue on Emotion and Decision Making)* 19, 2006, 115–137.

Libicki, M. C. and Pfleeger, S. L., "Collecting the Dots: Problem Formulation and Solution Elements," RAND Occasional Paper OP-103-RC, RAND Corporation, Santa Monica, CA, 2004.

Mack, A. and Rock, I., *Inattentional blindness*. Cambridge, MA: MIT Press, 1998.

Miller, G. A., "The Magical Number Seven, Plus or Minus Two: Some Limits on our Capacity for Processing Information," *Psychological Review*, 63, 1956, 81–97.

Pfleeger, S. L., Predd, J., Hunker, J., and Bulford, C., "Insiders Behaving Badly: Addressing Bad Actors and Their Actions," *IEEE Transactions on Information Forensics and Security* 5(2), March 2010.

Predd, J., Pfleeger, S. L., Hunker, J., and Bulford, C., "Insiders Behaving Badly," *IEEE Security and Privacy* 6(4), July/August 2008, 66–70.

Schneier, B., Semantic Attacks: The Third Wave of Network Attacks, 2000, https://www.schneier.com/crypto-gram/archives/2000/1015.html#1.

Simons, D. J. and Chabris, C. F., Gorillas in our Midst: Sustained Inattentional Blindness for Dynamic Events, Psychology, 1999.

Simons, D. J. and Jensen, M. S., *Psychonomic Bulletin & Review*, 16(2), 2009, 398–403.

3

THE CYBER PARADOX

Why More (of the Same) Is Less

Until now, we have focused on how technology, software, and quantitative applications are used in defense of the enterprise against cyberwarfare. The prevailing data point to the need for interim solutions until more robust cognitive defenses are developed. As the war in cyberspace escalates, comparisons are made that parallel the containment of the global arms race. Cyberwarfare presents even more formidable challenges. The dark web allows anyone who is highly motivated to develop skills to create or modify and use potentially destructive cyber weapons to damage infrastructure or cripple an industry with a level of anonymity not possible with conventional weapons.

Some leaders have called for a "cyber armistice" similar to nuclear nonproliferation treaties.* The United States and China met to discuss a sort of international détente on cyberwarfare. President Barack Obama and President Xi Jinping came together in the fall of 2015 in the first steps for establishing an agreement to refrain from using "cyber intrusions" to gain intellectual property between the two super powers. Whether the agreement is sustainable is questionable given the benefits of such actions; however, the unprecedented acknowledgment of the magnitude of cyberattacks by nation-states is remarkable.†

The rise of individual actors may preclude unilateral agreements between nations. Brazen hackers have become so confident that many have now implemented professional customer service models, making extortion as easy as any other online payment. In an April 2015 attack by hackers to extort the town of Tewksbury, Massachusetts with ransomware, hackers followed up with town officials, providing a document of FAQ (frequently asked questions) including instructions

---

* http://www.nytimes.com/2015/09/26/world/asia/xi-jinping-white-house.html?_r=0
† http://www.chinadaily.com.cn/cndy/2011-09/14/content_13680896.htm

for online payment.* Many of the attacks that implicate nation-states may be misdirected signals planted by lone wolf actors wanting to hide their tracks in cyberspace. The increasing sophistication of attacks suggests that cybercriminals are acting more like individual scientists in a lab who test vulnerabilities and collaborate by acting in unison or by selling modified versions in the black market, perpetuating the cycle of more effective and stealthy weapons.

In a recent survey, the top 10 countries with the most hackers were listed in order: China, United States, Turkey, Russia, Taiwan, Brazil, Romania, Italy, and Hungary. The numbers may be understated given the inability to validate the participants accurately. Each country had to represent at least 1% or greater of world attack traffic to make this list. In a study from Moscow-based Group-IB, Russia's share of the global cyber black market, estimated to be $12.5 billion, rose from $4.5 billion in 2011. On the other hand, Argentina has become a popular source of cyber talent in short supply of low-cost IT skills. Forrester Research estimated that outsources services in Latin America reached $8 billion in 2010 and has undoubtedly grown since then.†

According to a *New York Times* article in 2015 Argentina has become fertile recruiting ground for hackers for hire by business and governments seeking to defend against cybercrime.‡ Demand for security talent has driven Silicon Valley, government officials, and corporations to search worldwide, and Latin America's homegrown talent has demonstrated their skills are world class. One of the largest hacker conferences in Latin America, EkoParty, happens annually, with global attendees seeking to gain an edge. Argentina has put itself on the map as producing the best hackers while Brazil has developed a completely different reputation as the world leader in Internet banking fraud.

The *New York Times* article notes, "Technology companies like Apple, Facebook and Google have encrypted their products and services so that in many cases the only way to monitor a target's communications is to hack directly into its device. As a result, there is a

---

* http://www.reuters.com/article/us-usa-cyber-ransomware-idUSKCN0X917X
† http://www.cio.com/article/2415352/outsourcing/outsourcing--brazil-blossoms-as-it
  -services-hub.html
‡ http://www.nytimes.com/2015/12/01/technology/in-a-global-market-for-hacking
  -talent-argentines-stand-out.html?_r=0

new urgency among governments in acquiring zero-day exploits," an area of expertise for Argentine hackers. It is rumored that government officials, contractors, and spies are regular attendees of EkoParty each year to learn about the latest new products and best talent.

Latin America's hacker community also has a dark side that paints a disturbing picture of the future of cyber risks. Reporters from Bloomberg uncovered a story about Andrés Sepúlveda, a Colombia hacker, who is jailed on "charges including the use of malicious software, conspiracy to commit crime, violation of personal data, and espionage."* Sepúlveda has agreed to provide details about his exploits to reduce his sentence and gain public sympathy. But the real story behind Sepúlveda is the intriguing account of what he was doing and on whose behalf. Andrés claims that he and a team of hackers were hired to rig elections in Latin American countries including Nicaragua, Panama, Honduras, El Salvador, Colombia, Mexico, Costa Rica, Guatemala, and Venezuela. Andrés details how after watching the election results of President-elect Enrique Peña Nieto he "began destroying evidence. He drilled holes in flash drives, hard drives, and cell phones, fried their circuits in a microwave, then broke them to shards with a hammer. He shredded documents and flushed them down the toilet and erased servers in Russia and Ukraine rented anonymously with Bitcoins. He was dismantling what he says was a secret history of one of the dirtiest Latin American campaigns in recent memory."*

Andrés's team stole campaign strategies, manufactured social media accounts to fake public enthusiasm, and installed spyware against the opposition funded by a budget of more than half a million dollars by a Miami-based political consultant who admits to employing them to build a website but disavows knowledge of any dirty tricks. He was so successful he commented, "When I realized that people believe what the Internet says more than reality, I discovered that I had the power to make people believe almost anything."*

Sepúlveda is not the only hacker in Latin America to use his skills to go after politicians. "Two Peruvian hackers have broken into military, police, and other sensitive government networks in Argentina, Colombia, Chile, Venezuela, defacing websites and extracting

---

* http://www.bloomberg.com/features/2016-how-to-hack-an-election/

sensitive data to strut their programming prowess and make political points," according to a 2014 Associated Press (AP) report. The hackers also exposed members of Peru's Council of Ministers for influence peddling with the fishing and oil industry lobbies. Cyber hackers have also acted as whistleblowers on ethical behavior and freedom of speech where those rights have been suppressed. The dichotomy of the hacker community shows it is not a monolith following a predictive path. As the community gets larger and better skilled, each generation will build more powerful technology fueled by an influx of cash from both sides in warfare. In this environment, normal rules of engagement don't really apply. The asymmetry of risk in cyberspace requires intelligence to make sense of amorphous shifts in behavior. The Sepúlveda case demonstrates how alliances shift and change as hackers from both sides battle one another. Good cyber intelligence may be the only edge provided when parity is reached in a skill set.

The rules of the game change when secrets can be discovered and exposed by private contract hackers. Anonymous hackers have raised awareness by exposing security weakness and leaking embarrassing confidential data, putting governments on notice as in the case of the Panama Papers. Cyberspace is a double-edged sword cutting in both directions, where those with the best technology dictate the rules. Latin America is an example of a global community of hackers who have apprenticed with top talent and now have the skills to innovate their own tools to serve specific purposes. "This started out as hobbyists sharing exploits as a game," Mr. Arce said. "Now exploits are hoarded for profit."*

"Sale of a single exploit can make some hackers rich. Zerodium, a zero-day-exploit broker that sells to governments, said it paid hackers $1 million for an Apple exploit in October. In mid-November, the brokerage firm said it would pay hackers $50,000 for an attack that could take over a victim's machine through a Safari or Internet Explorer browser, and $80,000 for a similar attack through Google's Chrome browser," found by the *New York Times* article.

These stories reinforce why security analysts cannot rely on industry benchmarks to get an accurate assessment of threats in this

---

* http://www.nytimes.com/2015/12/01/technology/in-a-global-market-for-hacking
  -talent-argentines-stand-out.html?_r=0

environment. The backstory is important to put the pieces together and understand the complexity of each event as opposed to using generic threat reports that fail to shed light on the details. Cyber intelligence is a thriving business model but it is unclear what percentage is the type of threat reporting used in marketing as opposed to targeted intelligence reporting for higher-level threat analysis. Examples of advanced intelligence sharing between government agencies in the United States and Europe with security providers have taken place as early as 2012 but more is needed. High-level security clearance is required for intelligence sharing to become more comprehensive but does not preclude the IT community from considering the benefits of developing real-time intelligence on industry verticals through a self-regulatory association.*

Self-regulatory associations are one way to coordinate a range of cybersecurity initiatives aimed at improving the language of risk and agreeing on conventional and unconventional approaches to drive the agenda forward and fund initiatives on security. Some sectors have already started to share intelligence among groups of cohorts but that is not enough and cyber events in financial services can easily leak over to other groups. According to an industry report, "In a panel at the cybersecurity summit, Richard Davis, chairman and CEO of the U.S. Bank, explained how the Financial Services Information Sharing and Analysis Center (FS-ISAC) effort has helped protect the financial sector from cyberattacks. The concept of ISAC grew out of Presidential Decision Directive 63 (PDD-63) in 1998—which, much like the new directive signed by President Obama on Feb. 13, is about fostering collaboration and information sharing."† These efforts must be broader and better coordinated. These incremental solutions are partial solutions but don't address the strategic risk of cybercrime.

The market for cybersecurity is expected to grow to $170 billion by 2020, with increased investments in security and solutions fueled by recent attacks as well as the Internet of Things (IoT), which promises to expand the reach of the Internet more deeply into a growing

---

* http://breakinggov.com/2012/05/14/cyber-intelligence-sharing-intelligence-with
  -infrastructure-pro/
† http://www.eweek.com/security/the-paradox-of-todays-internet-and-cyber-security-2
  .html

list of new devices and endpoints unimaginable today. Advanced and emerging nations are investing heavily in security defense and likewise using cyberwarfare to counter threats similar to how nuclear defense is used to deter more aggressive behavior.

FBI Director James Comey, speaking at the Cybersecurity Law Institute at Georgetown Law Center on May 20, 2015, stated, "The threat we face has morphed. It's a chaotic spider web through social media—increasingly invisible to us because the operational communications are happening in an encrypted channel." The previously private conversations about the risk of attackers "going dark" described by the FBI as the use of encryption and other means to hide detection broke into the open recently in the now infamous but yet unresolved consequences of the case of the Apple iPhone used by the San Bernardino, California terror suspects. Comey summed up the problem thusly, "As all of our lives become digital, the logic of encryption in all of our lives will be covered by strong encryption, and therefore all of our lives—including the lives of criminals and terrorists and spies—will be in a place that is utterly unavailable to court-ordered process," he said. "And that, I think, to a democracy should be very, very concerning."*

In a 2013 report by the *Jerusalem Post*, Prime Minister Binyamin Netanyahu discussed building a "digital iron dome" at a ceremonial opening of a new national program to train young Israelis for cyberwarfare. "Israel's vital systems are under attack from Iran and other elements. This will only increase as we enter the digital age," Netanyahu stressed, speaking at the Ashkelon Academic College. Ashkelon College is one of many examples of classes and programs preparing a new generation of students for careers in cyber hacking. Understandably, the United States is also an active participant in developing young talent to close the gap of skills and innovation in cyberspace. In 2014, high school students gathered at the Hilton Coliseum in Ames, Iowa to compete in the 2014 IT-Olympics, sponsored by Iowa State University and the Technology Association of Iowa. This competition, along with other similar competitions taking place across the country, are part of an emerging grassroots effort to

---

* https://en.wikipedia.org/wiki/Alert_state; https://www.fbi.gov/news/news_blog
  /director-discusses-encryption-patriot-act-provisions

get young students interested in computer science, technology, engineering, and mathematics (STEM).

Private sector organizations are also responding to the growth in aspiring coders seeking more advanced skills. Black Hat Conference and its more hacker-oriented contemporary, DEFCON (an acronym for *defense readiness condition*), are some of the fastest growing conference and event organizers, providing training and a forum for networking with other coders. One of the more interesting sessions at DEFCON is called "Capture the Flag," where the contest winner demonstrated, in front of a large crowd, how he hacked into Walmart within 20 minutes. Underscoring how humans can represent a key vulnerability in security apparatus, this hacker was able to gain information about both physical security such as shift and break information and the type of computer systems and antivirus software that was displayed using one user's stolen account credentials.

As an aside, the founder of DEFCON and the Black Hat Conference, "Dark Tangent"/Jeff Moss, never accepts random LinkedIn connections, "I don't link to everyone who asks, I try to make sure I have met in person, or know of you through friends before I accept an invite." For those who are curious, DEFCON is a series of alert states coined by the U.S. Armed Forces, (5) being the least serious and (1) the most serious, to match various military situations.

Emerging nation-states are raising their game as well, such as, "North Korea has poured money into science and technology," according to a 2013 AP report. IT has become a buzzword in North Korea, which has developed its own operating system called Red Star. The regime also encouraged a passion for gadgets among its elite, introducing a Chinese-made tablet computer for the North Korean market. Teams of developers came up with software for everything from composing music to learning how to cook. But South Korea and the United States believe North Korea also has thousands of hackers trained by the state to carry its warfare into cyberspace, and their cyber offensive skills are as good as or better than those of their counterparts in China and South Korea.

"The newest addition to the North Korean asymmetric arsenal is a growing cyberwarfare capability," James Thurman, commander of the U.S. forces in South Korea, told U.S. legislators in March 2012.

"North Korea employs sophisticated computer hackers trained to launch cyber-infiltration and cyber-attacks" against South Korea and the United States. Much is at stake and it is hard to see where this ends as more powerful cyber weapons are developed. What is apparent is that cyberspace is threatened and the threat grows as other countries race to catch up with leaders in cyberspace.

Not surprisingly, the evidence to date points to humans or more accurately, human behavior on the web as the weak link. There is now more than a preponderance of evidence that our behavior or indifference to risk reinforces vulnerabilities to cyberattack. I call this "risk deafness." Discussions and awareness programs about risk are often ill-framed threats that occur so infrequently that listeners ignore them because the language is vague or lacks empowerment to identify the risk and act accordingly. We simply stop listening. Are we too complacent? Do we not understand the risks? Have we thrown in the towel suggested by some security professionals and consider cyberattacks a cost of doing business on the web? Security professionals need better tools to clarify risks and an understanding of the importance of human behavior when contemplating cyber defenses. Thankfully, there are insights to draw on from cognitive and behavioral science, such as Prospect theory and other research to assist in combating our own cognitive inertia to manage cyber risk.

Early collaborative work between Daniel Kahneman, noted for his work on the psychology of judgment and decision making as well as behavioral economics, and the cognitive and mathematical psychologist Amos Tversky focused on the psychology of prediction and probability judgment. Later they worked together to develop "Prospect theory," which aims to explain how people make decisions under risk and is considered one of the seminal works of behavioral economics. In the most cited paper in *Econometrica*, the prestigious academic journal of economics, Prospect theory (Kahneman and Tversky, 1981) redefined expected utility theory by proposing an alternative model. Kahneman and Tversky explained why people systemically err in simple and complex decision making.

These errors in judgment derive from personal heuristics, bias, or a lack of sufficient analytical skills. Prospect theory is an exhaustive look at how we make decisions under uncertain conditions.* A full analysis of Prospect theory is beyond the scope of this book, though there are concepts that have applicability to cybersecurity. Is Prospect theory, which is embedded in a branch of behavioral economics, relevant in understanding cybersecurity? Is it possible to improve cybersecurity through a better understanding of our own behavior and the behavior of others?

Kahneman and Tversky were not the first to explore how we make choices between uncertain outcomes; on the other hand, these researchers developed a more contemporary perspective with broader implications for decision making. In 2002, six years after Tversky's death, Kahneman won a Nobel Prize for the work he did in collaboration with Tversky (the Nobel is not awarded posthumously). The foundation of rational choice theories dates back to 1738, when Daniel Bernoulli first observed that humans made rational choices to optimize their outcomes. John von Neumann and Oskar Morganstern expanded Bernoulli's insights, which led to what Herbert Simon called a theory of "bounded rationality" in the nineteenth century. Kahneman and Tversky's contribution adds that we "regularly and systematically violate rational behavior at least some of the time and under certain conditions."† If this is true, how could Prospect theory be operationalized to reduce exposure to cyber risks?

Sheeri Lawrence Pfleeger, researcher at Dartmouth College's Institute for Information Infrastructure Protection, along with Deanna D. Caputo of the MITRE Corporation, explored the role cognition plays in developing more effective cybersecurity defense. Pfleeger and Caputo conducted an extensive review of behavioral science research on cybersecurity and discovered factors that lead to gaps in security. The studies focused on the importance and effectiveness of training as well as how to build better technology solutions.

Significant themes emerged from these studies related to the conscious and unconscious behaviors that lead to security weakness. Cognitive load is one of the key factors exhibited by employees and security professionals. Today's workforce is asked to do more with

---

* https://en.wikipedia.org/wiki/Amos_Tversky; https://en.wikipedia.org/wiki/Daniel _Kahneman
† https://hbr.org/2006/01/a-brief-history-of-decision-making

less, leaving employees stressed and overwhelmed by the velocity of change and volume of information each is responsible for in their organization. Staying on top of security protocols has become an obstacle to getting to the work that matters—growing revenues and satisfying customers—leaving some to override security or ignore the warnings of risk that appear remote to casual observers. Adding to the overload of data, corporate users must maintain several passwords to access multiple business systems while on the job or while traveling on business. Internal security policy requires users to change passwords periodically, adding to the burden of maintaining compliance with multiple systems and increasing cognitive load.

The promise of a single sign-on password across the enterprise is both technically challenging and presents segregation of duty conflicts when accessing highly sensitive internal data. Enterprise single sign-on has limited functionality in a workgroup environment in most organizations. Unfortunately, the cost and technical complexity of converting to a single domain is not reasonable in a business environment with multiple legacy systems from different vendors.

A Virginia Tech study found that "resistance behavior" increases even when users have been trained on the importance of security and consequences of not using strong passwords. Interestingly, the more technically competent the user is, the less compliant he or she is in adhering to the policies, suggesting that even IT professionals are equally likely to be the cause of weak security as compared to the rank-and-file employees when it comes to changing passwords frequently. The key is to find a balance for users in making security less disruptive and more intuitive that is integrated with real-time guidance (training).

As discussed earlier, trust is a major theme that runs through several behavioral research studies. The European Union conducted a multiyear, multidisciplinary project on online trust, called iTrust, documenting the ways trust can be created and broken when using the Internet. Designers of security systems have long recognized that a human-centered approach is needed to help users interface with technology more safely. New systems and security frameworks are being studied to take into account the human experience in design. Sasse and Flechais (2005) noted, "secure systems are socio-technical systems in which we should use an understanding of behavioral science to prevent users from being the 'weakest link'." Technological solutions are needed to support security analysts and reduce cognitive load by designing compliance and IT standards into operating environments. We must make security intuitive through system design and automate tasks that lead to better security outcomes for support staff.

The sociotechnical environment in which we now work, entertain ourselves, and find useful information is really an exchange between people facilitated by technology as opposed to face-to-face encounters. Trust is easier to determine when the interactions are face to face, or so we believe, but when human interactions are reduced to content and media the boundaries of trust are more malleable. Internet users assume trust exists when making a purchase online, using social media, or conducting research for a homework assignment. For the most part that is true, but we are seldom aware of those instances in which trust is violated on the Internet. This is where technology serves the biggest benefit through advanced algorithms to analyze content for threats. Likewise, a level of trust is expected in the designers of networked information systems; nevertheless expectations about security must become more explicit to prevent surprises.

Gaps in security were common from the beginning of network design; all the same, today's vulnerabilities leave organizations and consumers exposed to serious security threats. Design vulnerabilities are prime targets in cyberattacks called "zero-day threats," which are unknown to security professionals until a breach in security or alerts from infrastructure providers leave firms exposed to a breach. Zero-day threats are particularly easy to exploit by hackers who remotely send out botnets in search of these weaknesses. The time between detection of the vulnerability and mitigation is often several days, providing hackers with the opportunity to launch additional malware or steal confidential data. Given the serious threat posed by zero-day vulnerabilities security professionals should not wait for patch alerts from vendors but instead implement proactive vulnerability scans of their own to reduce gaps in time to patch, repair, or develop alternatives for these threats. Vulnerability management is a full-time job that requires a strategic approach and automation to support a security analyst's workload.

Choices in security are not unlike gambles with financial outcomes; these choices, whether selected by process or management, are considered optimal but are poorly framed without the benefit of formal analysis. Poor investment outcomes in security result in sunk costs that escalate as a cycle of informal decision making perpetuates even higher spending on layered security. The embedded problem in the cybersecurity paradox is an error most cybersecurity analysts make when selecting among available defensive postures. The problem is an "isolation error" labeled by Kahneman and Lovallo (1993), which consists of two biases that lead analysts astray. The first "forecasts of future outcomes are often anchored on plans and scenarios of success rather than on past results, and are therefore overly optimistic; and the second, their evaluations of single risky prospects neglect the possibilities of pooling risks and are therefore overly timid."*

The argument is that the balance of these two errors impacts decisions made by organizations and their choice in risk taking. The potential outcome is, "A decision maker who is risk averse in some situations and risk seeking in others ends up paying a premium to avoid some risks and a premium to obtain others. Because the outcomes are ultimately combined, these payments may be unsound." This partially explains why cybersecurity spending continues to escalate with little to no sustainable evidence in risk reductions. A less obvious reason is the "illusion of control." Several researchers have documented examples in which "managers commonly view risk as a challenge to be overcome, and believe that risk can be modified by "managerial wisdom and skill" (Donaldson and Lorsch, 1983). The common refusal of managers to refuse risk estimates provided to them as "given" (Shapira, 1986) is a clear illustration of "illusion of control."

The concept of making decisions under uncertainty is relevant to Internet users as well as others who must decide between risky choices. However, assessing risks in cyberspace is compounded by uncertainty, leading to confusion about an appropriate response. The cybersecurity paradox is a conundrum, "On one hand, the Internet has enabled an unparalleled era of innovation and collaboration. On the other, the Internet has also enabled attackers to cross nation-state borders at will in the digital realm and impact Americans."† There are

---

* http://courses.washington.edu/pbafhall/514/514%20Readings/TimidChoicesAnd
  BoldForecasts.pdf
† http://www.eweek.com/security/the-paradox-of-todays-internet-and-cyber-security
  .html

skeptics of the cybersecurity paradox, with some believing the hype of "Cybergeddon" is overdone. "The first clear step towards cyber-sanity is directing the enormous governmental and extra-governmental cyber apparatus towards measurable, clear goals. As [David] Auerbach (software engineer and Slate columnist) says, outsiders must carry out unsparing audits of key agencies and systems, and the government should use such problems to solve quantifiable, measurable problems that it actually has."*

Security is considered secondary to users seeking to conduct their business on the Internet. The concept of trust is a relative risk taken. In these situations of inattentional blindness we are vulnerable to cognitive hacks. Hackers are also smart consumers of research and understand the role trust plays on the Internet. A 2012 finding by Symantec discovered that hackers have transitioned from porn sites to church websites and Christian and youth forums now equally or more likely to contain malware.

Symantec, the maker of Norton™ Antivirus software, found that "religious and ideological sites" have far surpassed pornographic websites as targets for criminal hackers.† Hackers have become astute in cloaking their attack vectors, described as malvertisement, in previously trustworthy media and content. Adobe PDF files have also become a common entry point as well as video, advertisements, and other media. The proliferation of new approaches for launching an attack via Internet content means that literally very little content is safe even on trusted websites of established organizations. Computer-assisted monitoring is needed to enhance situational awareness to recognize anomalies in behavior *after* malware has been activated.

We have already explored the concept of *cognitive load* and *inattentional blindness* but it is important to point out both are key factors that limit our ability to recognize the subtleties of evolving threats. The findings propose that security analysts are ill equipped to fully grasp the changing nature of cyber risk or connect the dots as information unfolds in nonlinear patterns. Technology is evolving but is not sufficient at this time for handling the asymmetric nature of cyber risk,

---

* http://www.businessinsider.com/the-opm-breachs-cybersecurity-paradox-2015-6
† http://www.slate.com/articles/technology/technology/2012/05/malware_and _computer_viruses_they_ve_left_porn_sites_for_religious_sites_.html

so how does behavioral science enhance security and improve risk management?

The context for understanding why cognitive hacks are so effective starts with an understanding of our own bias and ability to make an honest assessment of the inherent limitations for processing information that is not familiar. Let's first take a look at the behavioral science findings that limit our ability to connect the dots in cybersecurity and then build the case for improving our awareness of bias and cognitive load to design more effective risk management programs.

Humans are optimistic to a fault! Optimism is what drives us to succeed against all odds and serves as the basis for innovation and our greatest achievement. We build on success and learn incrementally from success and failure. Unfortunately, failure is far more likely than success but we choose to limit or diminish our failures in light of the odds and recall successes as more highly probable. A 2014 Global State of Information Security Survey conducted by PriceWaterhouseCoopers and CSO Online found that 73% of security executives are quite confident of the effectiveness of their security programs even though 82% of a sample of 460 companies had been found with observable compromise the year before.*

A separate Booz Allen Hamilton and Frost and Sullivan study in 2013, ISC2, found a vast majority of respondents were confident that their organization would perform better or the same relative to 2012.† Lastly, a 2014 Trustwave Security Pressures Report found 72% of respondents feel safe from IT security threats. Sixty percent of the respondents were CIOs, CISOs, VPs, and directors. In contrast, a PwC 2016 Global Information Security Study showed that IT security budgets have risen by 24%, "hard" intellectual property theft is up 56%, incidents of compromise related to business partners has risen 22%, and 38% more cyber incidents were reported over the previous year. The incentives for managing cybersecurity should be reconsidered. Increased spending is not an accurate measure of better risk management or security protection. The laws of diminishing return apply equally in cybersecurity and risk management.

---

* http://www.pwc.com/gx/en/issues/cyber-security/information-security-survey.html
† https://www.isc2cares.org/uploadedFiles/wwwisc2caresorg/Content/2013-ISC2
  -Global-Information-Security-Workforce-Study.pdf

It is human nature to be optimistic about one's own performance yet less optimistic about that of others. Hard data are also not incentive enough to change behavior. Corporate inertia is a major factor in dealing with cybersecurity. Let's face it, survival requires an optimistic outlook and, comparatively speaking, performance in cybersecurity is relative. Behavioral science is useful in the context of cyber risk in that it provides security professionals with a new set of tools to frame the conversation about the probability of cyberattacks as well as the preparations for addressing it when and if it occurs.

Conversations about cyber risk with senior management and boards of directors must be reframed through a formal dialogue that matures from simple awareness campaigns to quantitative distributions of possibilities and finally to execution. Cybersecurity is not a one-size-fits-all program, but a transition to customization requires a framework with clear outcomes and measureable parameters that lead to increased trust in networked information systems. The concept of risk is not at all as intuitive as many believe and cyber risk may be the least intuitive risk faced by all organizations today. If humans are the weakest link in cybersecurity then it stands to reason that the quality of our decisions to address threats in cyberspace will either strengthen or weaken the link.

Models for building trust into system applications is a concept that dates to a 1977 publication by Kenneth J. Biba, considered a refinement of the Bell-LaPadula Model, a classical model used to define access control. In the "Biba Integrity Model," a "system of computer security policies expressed as access control rules is designed to ensure data integrity.* The model defines a hierarchy of integrity levels and then prevents participants from corrupting data of an integrity level higher than the subject, or from being corrupted by data from a level lower than the subject." Biba's Integrity Model makes a distinction between "integrity" and "trustworthiness" (security).† The Biba model is generally thought to be a simple integrity model addressing only the protection of the system from access by unauthorized users while ignoring availability and confidentiality. A competing model, the Clark–Wilson Integrity Model, created 10 years later in 1987 is

---

* http://link.springer.com/referenceworkentry/10.1007%2F978-1-4419-5906-5_774
† https://en.wikipedia.org/wiki/Biba_Model

a more robust model that dictates the enforcement of separation of duties; subjects must access data through an application; and auditing is required.* The Clark–Wilson Integrity Model is concerned with formalizing the notion of information integrity. "Information integrity is maintained by preventing corruption of data items in a system due to either error or malicious intent. An integrity policy describes how the data items in the system should be kept valid from one state of the system to the next and specifies the capabilities of various principals in the system."*

New cyber trust models are emerging along various points of view based on either data traffic or network infrastructure. One example is the Forrester Research's "Zero-Trust Model" for cybersecurity; Forrester assumes that all traffic is untrusted.† The Zero-Trust Model is based on three fundamental principles: (1) Assume all traffic is untrusted and verify all traffic is encrypted, authorized, inspected, and secured. (2) Enforce a policy of minimal privileges and strict access control. (3) Inspect and log all traffic.

Cisco's Trust Model is based on defending network architecture. Cisco also uses a three-point program that is internally focused on network trust.‡ Network trust framework alignment is defined as (1) Asset Discovery and Management—validation of user and device identity; (2) Configuration Management and Remediation— identify misconfigurations and vulnerabilities; and (3) Architecture Optimization—enhance design and feature applications for a resilient, threat-resistant infrastructure.

Forrester's Zero-Trust Model is partly aspirational owing to a lack of existing technology and an absence of the components to operationalize the model. Cisco, on the other hand, represents a more traditional approach focused on monitoring and securing the network. There is no "golden ticket" to a cybersecurity trust model; however, general agreement exists on encryption, authentication, and authorization as core to all models. These fundamental areas have remained sacrosanct over two or more decades of information security but do

---

* https://en.wikipedia.org/wiki/Clark%E2%80%93Wilson_model
† http://csrc.nist.gov/cyberframework/rfi_comments/040813_forrester_research.pdf
‡ http://www.cisco.com/c/dam/en_us/solutions/industries/docs/gov/cybersecurity _bvr_wp.pdf

not explain why today's trust model(s) provide less trust than expected against cybercrime.

These divergent trust models illustrate how "trust" is relative to a security professional's preference, experience, security practice, and infrastructure. Neither model fully anticipates how humans engage technology, which partly explains why the cybersecurity paradox persists. "An Associated Press review of the $10 billion-a-year federal effort to protect sensitive data shows that the government struggles to close holes without the knowledge, staff or systems to keep pace with increasing attacks by an ever-evolving and determined foe.* Last year (2013), for example, about 21 percent of all federal breaches were traced to government workers who violated policies; 16 percent who lost devices or had them stolen; 12 percent who improperly handled sensitive information printed from computers; at least 8 percent who ran or installed malicious software; and 6 percent who were enticed to share private information, according to an annual White House review."

The Forrester Research and Cisco Systems' Trust Model(s) demonstrate why a program directed at data and/or infrastructure alone proves to be less than effective. The integrity and trust of any organization's network must anticipate the risk of employee behavior beyond the insider threat characterized by many programs. When employees bypass corporate policy, whether intentional or not, the employee's firm is vulnerable to the proverbial "Trojan horse," defeating many of the good intentions designed in trust models.

Employee behavior trumps a firm's policies and procedures no matter how stringent the enterprise security program. In a speech to industry leaders, former FBI director Robert Mueller described an incident whereby someone with years of security experience received an email requesting that he update his personal information with his bank. On clicking on the link and starting, but not finishing, he had second thoughts and later learned that he almost became a victim of a phishing expedition. The person in question was the FBI director himself—someone who knows better and should have recognized the ploy but was tricked by a cognitive hack.

---

* http://newsbusters.org/blogs/joseph-rossell/2015/02/26/fcc-passes-regulations
  -enabling-government-micromanage-internet

We are all susceptible. Employees are not to blame! Many organizations provide access to social media sites, external email, and Internet surfing from company computers. The insider threat really is a self-inflicted wound caused by the absence of a cogent approach to delivering the right balance of freedom and security. Corporations err on the side of more freedom, assuming "more" is better. Security analysts must begin to ask harder questions. How can we make security simple, intuitive? What is really required to get our jobs done? What is a convenience versus a necessity to get one's job done? What alternatives are available to facilitate a mobile workforce in an intuitive, secure environment? To build security for humans we must ask these and many more questions to address the cybersecurity paradox. A consensus has been reached that "we humans" are the weak link yet we are reluctant to change because we trust technology less than we do ourselves.*

Businesses will pursue eCommerce as long as the benefits outweigh the costs; on the other hand, if costs rise faster than revenues the model eventually fails. Researchers have suggested that the net present value of information security adds value through risk mitigation.[†] What observers fail to capture in this analysis is a comparison of the difference in the rate of growth in spending on cybersecurity and the lost opportunity of investing in alternative strategies with a higher present value. The cybersecurity paradox clearly points to a minimal, even negative net present value from cybersecurity as security pros continue falling behind.

The alternatives may first appear to be drastic on the surface, such as offering less user choice and less freedom within organizational environments as management considers the appropriate tradeoffs for increased security. Network architecture redesign must consider human behavior inclusive of security and beyond that ways to optimize simplicity. This forward-looking approach is called a Cognitive Risk Framework for Cybersecurity.

A Cognitive Risk Framework for Cybersecurity is discussed in detail later; nevertheless, the core pillars of the program include

---

* http://www.govtech.com/opinion/Cybersecuritys-Weakest-Link-Humans.html
† http://www.developer.com/tech/article.php/640831/Net-Present-Value-of
  -Information-Security-Part-I.htm

Security Informatics, Anticipatory/Intuitive Architecture Design, Decision-Support Analytics, and Cognitive Risk Awareness and Training as well as cross-disciplinary concepts still in development. A cognitive risk framework must complement existing security over time by making security intuitive and simple. IT budgets must be shaped around strategic enterprise risk informed by data and designed to solve specific problems, not assess the entire organization. You will know you have arrived at the right balance when compliance is as intuitive as using a smartphone. It is naive to expect every person in the organization to "own" risk. No one knows what it means or how to make it a reality. The objective is to narrow the "corridor of vulnerability" as the Greek general Leonidas did at the narrow pass of Thermopylae in defending Athens from an invading Persian army. Leonidas did not survive the attack but gave his Greek citizens additional time to evacuate before the arrival of the larger Persian army.*

Cybercrime continues unabated in the face of a long history of trust models; therefore a more nuanced look at trust must be undertaken to help understand what is happening. Before we get into the weeds it may be helpful here to take a bird's eye view of cybersecurity from the perspective of the World Wide Web.

Should users of the Internet expect a certain level of cybersecurity to be in place or embedded into the Internet? Does the Internet have a governance framework for cybersecurity? It turns out that a dedicated network of nonprofit associations governs the World Wide Web.

The World Wide Web is one area of commerce where government regulation has not actively intervened but that may be changing.† The FBI case against Apple to unlock the smartphone of the San Bernardino terrorists is just one example of how tensions have been building over security, privacy, and government oversight. As the Internet continues to grow and contribute a larger share of global GDP, growth issues of national security may force change in the government's role in regulating eCommerce.‡ Net neutrality is the first shot over the bow but certainly not the last. Federal Communications

---

* http://urgentcomm.com/blog/attraction-and-training-keys-developing-cybersecurity
  -talent
† http://newsbusters.org/blogs/joseph-rossell/2015/02/26/fcc-passes-regulations
  -enabling-government-micromanage-internet
‡ https://www.whitehouse.gov/net-neutrality

Commission (FCC) Chairman Tom Wheeler said the Internet was "simply too important to be left without rules and a referee on the field." In contrast, Republican FCC commissioner Ajit Pai, a vocal critic of the plan and one of the votes against it, said the FCC was "turning its back on Internet" because "President Obama told us to do so."

The FCC did, however, adopt the "Open Internet" rules on February 26, 2015, which went into effect June 12, 2015.* "An Open Internet means consumers can go where they want, when they want. This principle is often referred to as Net Neutrality. It means innovators can develop products and services without asking for permission. It means consumers will demand more and better broadband as they enjoy new lawful Internet services, applications and content, and broadband providers cannot block, throttle, or create special 'fast lanes' for that content. The FCC's Open Internet rules protect and maintain open, uninhibited access to legal online content without broadband Internet access providers being allowed to block, impair, or establish fast/slow lanes to lawful content."*

Unfortunately, the debate over regulating the Internet has failed to include a discussion for how to ensure protections from cybercrime on the World Wide Web. "The Internet was built for openness and speed, not for cybersecurity. John Doyle's 'Robust Yet Fragile' description of the Internet is even more relevant today than ever before. As more and more services, infrastructure and personal information move online, they have all become targets for hackers, who constantly scan the Internet for potential security holes and entry points. Security experts say there is no way to keep hackers out of systems with traditional defenses like firewalls and antivirus software," according to a July 29, 2015 *New York Times* article.[†]

"No one person, company, organization or government runs the Internet. It is a globally distributed network comprising many voluntarily interconnected autonomous networks. It operates without a central governing body with each constituent network setting and enforcing its own policies. A decentralized and international

---

* https://www.fcc.gov/general/open-internet

† http://www.nytimes.com/interactive/2015/07/29/technology/personaltech/what
  -parts-of-your-information-have-been-exposed-to-hackers-quiz.html?_r=0

multistakeholder network of interconnected autonomous groups drawing from civil society, the private sector, governments, the academic and research communities and national and international organizations conducts its governance. They work cooperatively from their respective roles to create shared policies and standard that maintains the Internet's global interoperability for the public good."* To grasp the magnitude of global human collaboration to support and maintain the Internet see Figure 3.1.

This graphic is a living document, designed to provide a high-level view of how the Internet is run. It is not intended to be a definitive guide.

Managing the global network of the web requires coordination on a massive scale. Much of the interoperability, technical, and policy aspects of the core underpinnings and naming protocols are administered by the Internet Corporation for Assigned Names and Numbers (ICANN), which is headquartered in Los Angeles, California. An international board of directors drawn from across the Internet's technical, business, academic, and other noncommercial communities governs ICANN.

"The National Telecommunications and Information Administration (NTIA), an agency of the United States Department of Commerce, has exercised ultimate authority over the DNS root zone of the Internet since it was transitioned into private hands in 1997 (Brito, 2011; Farivar, 2014). In March 2014, the NTIA announced that it will cede this authority to an organization whose nature has yet to be specified."

While ICANN itself interpreted this as a declaration of its independence, scholars still point out that this is not yet the case. Considering that the U.S. Department of Commerce can unilaterally terminate the Affirmation of Commitments with ICANN, the authority of DNS administration is likewise seen as revocable and derived from a single state, namely the United States. The technical underpinning and standardization of the Internet's core protocols (IPv4 and IPv6) is an activity of the Internet Engineering Task Force (IETF), a nonprofit organization of loosely affiliated international participants that anyone may join by contributing technical expertise.

---

* https://en.wikipedia.org/wiki/Internet_governance

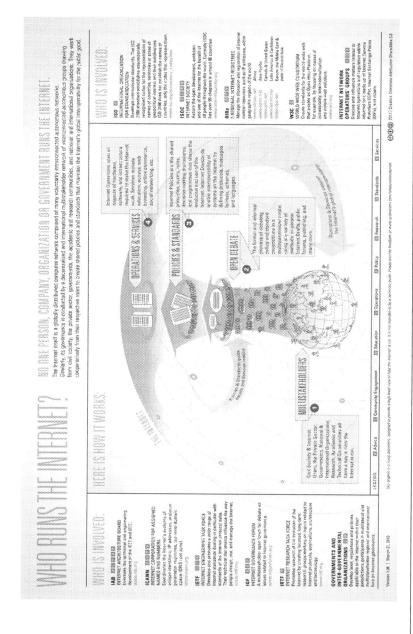

Figure 3.1 Who runs the Internet. *Source:* Wikipedia, https://www.wikipedia.org.

Yet another nonprofit group called the World Wide Web Consortium (W3C) works collaboratively to provide guidance and principles for using the web. W3C is an international community that develops open standards to ensure the long-term growth of the web. Anyone can join and support W3C's mission, which operates under a Code of Ethics and Professional Conduct.* The W3C's mission is to lead the World Wide Web to its full potential by developing protocols and guidelines that ensure the long-term growth of the W3C's vision of One Web.† W3C is founded on two basic principles: an open Standards principle—an open and collectively empowering model that will help radically improve the way people around the world develop new technologies and innovate for humanity; and design principles that include Web for All—accessibility as a right to everyone in the world to connect and share for the benefit of humanity—and Web on Everything, which includes devices, mobile technology, browsers, and other agents. The W3C vision encompasses web design and architecture; web data and services; and a web of trust, security, and privacy. The W3C's altruistic mission is threatened by three dynamic forces intersecting simultaneously with conflicting agendas: cybercrime, eCommerce business, and sovereign government security each attempting to assume more control over the openness and accessibility of the Internet.

Surprisingly, no one organization, governmental agency, or consortium is directly responsible for ensuring cybersecurity for the World Wide Web.‡ Therefore, each of us and every organization have a shared responsibility for security and privacy. A shared responsibility for cybersecurity is also embodied in the collective actions at the human–machine intersection but more is needed to make these interactions intuitive and simple. Now more than ever, each of us creates an *intricate digital footprint* that serves to either preserve or threaten the survival of the web. Tim Berners-Lee's World Wide Web was launched as a trusted service designed to benefit humanity. Ironically, trust is the biggest threat to the future of the web.

---

* https://www.w3.org/support/
† https://www.w3.org/Consortium/mission
‡ http://www.nationaldefensemagazine.org/archive/2011/June/Pages/Whois ResponsibleforCybersecurity.aspx

In a real-life example of how choice determines success or failure let's look at a very simple story recently published in Bloomberg.* The general manager of a small medical testing lab in Atlanta, Georgia received a phone call in May 2008 from a gentleman claiming he had a file of the lab's patient information. Protecting medical records is a critical requirement for all healthcare providers and subject to Health Insurance Portability and Accountability Act (HIPAA) regulatory scrutiny. To prove the breach was real the caller emailed a sample of the records to the CEO, Michael Daugherty. As it turned out, the person calling was seeking to use the breach to sell his services of security remediation to the medical lab. The implied threat was that if Mr. Daugherty did not comply with the caller's request to pay for his services the breach would be reported to governmental agencies. Cyber extortion is not new but this behavior is extremely troublesome.

Mr. Daugherty resisted the threats and by January 2010 the Federal Trade Commission (FTC)'s Division of Privacy and Identity Protection started an inquiry into the alleged breach, after it presumably had been reported by the extortionist. After months of attempting to address the FTC's inquiry the investigation took a bad turn when Mr. Daugherty decided to resist settling the case like so many of the other firms that had also been ensnared in the extortionist's trap. "The FTC has a dual mandate: to protect consumers and to promote competition. Its protective powers are laid out in Section 5 of the Federal Trade Commission Act, which prohibits 'unfair or deceptive acts or practices in or affecting commerce.' The FTC also applies Section 5 to information security, casting careless handling of consumers' information as a form of unfair and deceptive business practices. The FTC reached its first settlement in this area in 2000, with a group of online pharmacies over their collection and use of customer information. Since then, the commission has brought more than 60 cases related to data security. In all but one, the companies involved have settled, signing consent decrees that in many cases require 20 years of security audits by an outside firm and sometimes fines.† The alternative

---

* http://www.bloomberg.com/features/2016-labmd-ftc-tiversa/
† http://www.bloomberg.com/news/articles/2013-03-05/protecting-privacy-on-the -internet

is litigation, which the FTC can initiate in federal court or in its own administrative court system."*

The one company that did not settle with the FTC was Mr. Daugherty's. The path of least resistance is to settle; however, Mr. Daugherty decided to stand on principle and pursue his case and fight the FTC. After several years of legal battles with the FTC, Mr. Daugherty's case had a surprising ending. An insider at Tiversa, the extortionist's firm, admitted to the fraud. In addition, the FTC's case proved to be an abuse of governmental authority and hubris that relied solely on the evidence provided by Tiversa. During the case, an investigative report revealed an ongoing relationship between Tiversa and the FTC dating back to 2007 in which dozens of firms were fraudulently accused. This case is precedent setting for a number of reasons, not the least of which is that some government agencies are ill prepared to effectively oversee cyber cases involving cognitive hacks used by unscrupulous actors, nor are there sufficient legal rulings to establish fact patterns to properly examine the implications of cyber fraud in this form.

Michael Daugherty was finally vindicated in his efforts but not before filing for bankruptcy; losing his firm and clients; and at middle age, seeking to start over because of one small error in judgment that many firms overlook. An employee in the billing department of the medical lab had been using LimeWire, the file-sharing website, to download music. Without knowing it she'd left her document file with the insurance report open for sharing on the LimeWire peer-to-peer network for others to see. This behavior was a violation of company policy. Tiversa used a proprietary search engine it had developed to scour peer-to-peer networks looking for information to use in their extortion efforts and found the medical lab's data.

Mr. Daugherty and his security team are as much at fault as Tiversa in the failure of his firm. Corporations that allow Internet surfing during business hours create the opportunity for breaches to occur, and worse, the loss of confidential and private personal identifiable information. Corporate policies are ineffective as deterrents when policies do not take into account human behavior. There are

---

* https://www.ftc.gov/about-ftc/what-we-do/enforcement-authority

few justifiable reasons left for corporations to allow open Internet access given the broad use of smartphones. I would add that the push to add "Bring Your Own Device," or BYOD, is an equally unwise security move by large firms to accommodate millennial employees who want access all the time but frequently use it for non-business purposes. To date, cybersecurity has primarily assumed a "defense and respond" posture with increasing investment in assets, capability, and technology with diminishing returns in risk mitigation. Surprisingly, the greatest potential for increased security may lie in the least expense targeted at employee behavior. Choice is an option with attached risks and benefits, measured against a matrix of security threats. The best security may be the choice to NOT do more of the same.

In his book *The Paradox of Choice*, Barry Schwartz (2004) explains how as the number of choices increase our level of anxiety grows. The counterintuitive finding is that "too many choices hamper decision-making and clouds judgment," increasing vulnerability. The vastness of the Internet is the ultimate in an endless stream of choice of content from news and information, entertainment to social interactions, resulting in increased exposure to cognitive hacks. The Fear of Missing Out (FOMO) is a new reality in an endless stream of online media now frequently "trended" by mainline media or shared as gossip with friends and acquaintances on social media sites. "Why More Is Less" defined by the proliferation of social media sites captures the essence of why cognitive hacks are so effective, leaving Internet users more vulnerable than ever to cyberattack.

According to a Dell SecureWorks incident report, "instead of using phishing and malware attackers gained access to a large manufacturer's server responsible for sending out security updates to all endpoints in the company. Instead of patching the system, the attackers used the updated software to execute commands allowing them to obtain additional credentials."* Incidents like these demonstrate the challenge of responding to past incidents while being exposed to existing vulnerabilities that have yet to be discovered or adequately addressed.

---

* http://www.infoworld.com/article/2983774/security/attackers-go-on-malware-free
  -diet.html

Current defense posture falls short in responding to the speed of change as cyberattackers adjust to new defense tactics more quickly.

These warnings have been sounded before with very little change in behavior, which is the very definition of risk deafness. *Risk deafness* is different from *risk blindness* in terms of how we experience risks. Risk blindness is the result of little to no knowledge of a risk until faced with a decision that results in a loss or physical harm. Risk deafness is subtle and deals with one's belief in the warnings of a risk not yet experienced or a belief that the risk will happen to someone else. Risk deafness and risk blindness represent degrees of the same error in judgment about the occurrence of a risk and the actual impact experienced by a person or organization. This phenomenon can be seen in how people respond to warnings about imminent natural disasters, such as hurricanes, and other events. This is also why threat warnings or training about a host of risks fail to substantially change behavior permanently. Constant warnings about infrequent risk events with varying degrees of impact create cognitive dissonance.* "Leon Festinger's theory of cognitive dissonance focuses on how humans strive for internal consistency. An individual who experiences inconsistency (dissonance) tends to become psychologically uncomfortable, and is motivated to try to reduce this dissonance—as well as actively avoid situations and information likely to increase it."* Risk deafness and risk blindness are terms that I have created to help explain these observations.

More choice does not appear to improve security effectiveness in physical security nor reduce the exposure to attack in cyberattacks. The influence asserted by friends and family on social media sites outweighs the perceived risk of a cyberattack. The American ethos of freedom to choose limits how much change can be implemented systemically to solve the growing problem of cyber hacks. A market economy and the free enterprise system drive providers to offer multiple versions of new content. The push for new markets in technology and on the web will usher in new wealth models but conversely expose us to even greater risks. Projections of trillion dollar opportunities in new market categories, such as the IoT, may also usher in even greater vulnerabilities ideally suited to the creative energies of

---

* https://en.wikipedia.org/wiki/Cognitive_dissonance

hackers. The tradeoff between convenience and security encapsulates varying degrees of risk deafness and risk blindness in ways that we are incapable of predicting today. We have already seen some signs as red flags are being ignored as industry rushes forward in a push to connect devices without equal considerations for security to protect consumers. Not everyone agrees that increased choice is a problem.

The correlation between cyberattacks and social media does not suggest causation but also doesn't discount the linkage either. There is, however, growing evidence of the correlation between the two. Research on social media cyber forensics is scarce but a study (Al Matuwa et al., 2011) in the 2011 International Conference for Internet Technology and Secured Transactions (ICITST) demonstrated an ability to identify groups of cyberattackers in social media with a high degree of accuracy.* Social media has become a trusted source of information for Internet surfers while paradoxically representing one of the greatest vulnerabilities in cyberspace.

Cybersecurity risk management requires a formalized approach for choosing between convenience and business critical exposures. When the cost of convenience exceeds the benefits to business critical functionality *choice* should be minimized. How would this work? Reduce the "Corridor of Vulnerability": restrict access to social media sites, external cloud repositories, email, and enforce encryption where possible. Finally, limit Internet access by employees beyond business critical functions with trusted partners, and establish secure portals for conducting business.

Security is a choice between a range of possible scenarios each with a distribution of probabilities. In the vast majority of cases, security professionals are ill prepared to accurately determine the most likely scenario(s) or the distribution of probabilities due to insufficient data or a lack of the requisite skills to make the calculations.

The behavioral sciences offer some guidance for understanding how ill prepared we are when making decisions under uncertain conditions. Too often these decisions are made using intuition, past experience (short-term memory), or tradeoffs between expediency and costs. Unknowingly, strategic decision makers rely on heuristics in judging when attempting to apply solutions from the past to solve new

---

* http://journalsweb.org/siteadmin/upload/56864%20IJRET014045.pdf

problems. The fallacy takes shape in the form of poorly constructed arguments used to support a decision that relies on faulty reasoning. Intertemporal choice is the study of why we consistently make poor choices when faced with uncertainty. Decisions about work effort, choosing a spouse, saving for the future, dieting, budget planning, and risk management are examples of intertemporal choice.

These choices have consequences over multiple time periods, and most involve making a choice among various options with a great deal of uncertainty predicting future outcomes. Organizations take for granted the incremental cost of poor decisions because they are seldom tallied or attributed to decision makers unless the loss is substantial. The result is a hidden legacy of bad decision making that, left unaddressed, can easily become tail risks that eventually threaten organizational effectiveness. Formalizing choice becomes increasingly important as the consequences of poor decision making become more obvious.

Researchers have determined that the choices we make are the result of the discount factors we use when choosing between outcomes. For example, high discount rates are attributed to self-gratification and short-term benefits.* Low discount rates are attributed to choices involving planning for the future and making investments in payoffs over many years. When choosing between receiving $100 today versus receiving $125 one year from now we often choose to take the $100 now.* The decision to forego a 25% return by not waiting is considered a high discount rate. If you choose to wait one year to receive the higher return you are said to possess a low discount rate. Individuals with lower discount rates (willing to sacrifice or postpone self-gratification) are considered to have higher cognitive abilities and make more optimal choices. This description may seem harsh but is used to differentiate how utility theory is exercised in choosing between optimal outcomes.

Businesses have developed a variety of ways, both formal and informal, for choosing among business objectives. Financial budgeting is one of the predominant ways a business selects among its initiatives. Within the budgeting framework, these choices are screened using return on investment or other financial criteria including qualitative

---

* https://en.wikipedia.org/wiki/Intertemporal_choice

and quantitative methods. Risk management, and more specifically, cyber risk, doesn't easily fit into the normal budget boxes, resulting in less than adequate consultations about appropriate security outcomes.

Security professionals are left with few options then to demonstrate the value of security and risk management processes sans an actual cyber crisis. One common fallacy management makes is using "negative confirmation" or infrequent risk failures such as a cyber breach as evidence that security controls are working as expected or ineffective. If a security breach does happen and internal controls fail to prevent a breach the firm is subjected to reputational risk and financial repercussions in lost customer confidence and excessive overspending to remediate the gap. This leaves the security professional with a zero-sum game. Additional investments in security have become the default choice because more security is perceived better than less and is easier to justify. Defending against each known attack results in a spiraling escalation of security spending without an in-depth understanding of risk reduction. Some observers have attempted unsuccessfully to justify additional spending on cybersecurity using return on investment criteria. Cybersecurity investments, like any risk expense considerations, must be more targeted and specific around reductions in risk achieved. Risk reduction must be measureable as an end goal, with demonstrable reductions in the marginal cost of security one of several benefits achieved in the residual.

The narrative in the stories highlighted in this book suggests a root cause that runs through each event that points to a need for an enhanced view of defensive and offensive posture involving human cognitive factors in cybersecurity. Security must be reframed in terms of enterprise and cognitive outcomes to limit exposure to internal control failure. Cybersecurity must be repositioned to facilitate business execution and reduce risk through a well-articulated framework. The added benefit is that these same tools can be repurposed to assist organizations to evaluate organizational effectiveness through real-time intelligence. Enterprise risk has always been positioned as a strategic outcome in corporate governance. Advances in machine learning and artificial intelligence will link enterprise risk and business execution in ways not possible today, allowing boards to envision a future that can be modeled and acted upon with greater confidence.

Industry cyber threat reports point to diminishing returns in security spending, confirming the cybersecurity paradox. Even security pros acknowledge that layered security is leading to a tipping point in cyber defense, increasing the fragility of the enterprise as opposed to reducing risk. In addition, policies and procedures are important but the evidence is clear that transactional processes alone do not mitigate risks. Faced with these consequences, how should security professionals adjust their posture to account for decision risk?

Cognitive (decision) science is the scientific grounding for the development of machine learning and artificial intelligence in cybersecurity. System architects should leverage these concepts when considering how to redesign internal controls (policy and procedures) into systems, creating an intuitive, less intrusive human interface to reduce the corridor of vulnerability. Cognitive science enables security professionals to build trust models into applications and anticipate errors in human judgment. Cyber intelligence guided by a cognitive risk framework for cybersecurity provides a path to an enhanced cybersecurity program. The theory of "discounted utility" is one of many concepts available in intertemporal choice models that serve as a basis for understanding new approaches to refine defensive strategy. To understand how this works one must begin with the science of choice. Choice is more than "thinking outside the box." These concepts completely redesign the box in new ways that have traditionally limited progress in risk management. So what is the science of choice?

What is intertemporal choice? Intertemporal choice is defined as "decisions with consequences that play out over time—these choices are important and ubiquitous"* at all organizations. Intertemporal choice is one of the foundational concepts used in cognitive risk and should be understood by security and risk professionals interested in building more sustainable frameworks for managing risk.*

Operationally, intertemporal choice involves making decisions, some with high utility and others with low utility for the decision maker. Decision makers with high utility are typically described as seekers of immediate gratification. For example, when asked to choose between receiving $100 now versus $125 in one year, high-utility

---

* https://dash.harvard.edu/bitstream/handle/1/4554332/Laibson_Intertemporal Choice.pdf

decision makers want $100 now. Low-utility decision makers are willing to wait one year for the additional money. The magnitude of the reward may vary the decision and these decisions evolve over time; however, generally speaking, the preceding examples describe how choices are made. Researchers blame high discount rates for our generalized failure to save enough for retirement or stay with diets, or for our propensity to spend more time planning vacations than we do preparing for old age.

Intertemporal choice depends in large part on a person's ability to understand optimal choices by employing a set of disciplines to weigh the outcome of benefits and risks of decisions. Intertemporal choice presumes that individuals with appropriate analytical skills, such as Bayesian probability, will possess low discount rates and ultimately make more informed choices; however, choice can be affected by influences in the environment that change over time. These influences may have the effect of increasing one's discount rate. For example, if a security professional has recently experienced a serious data breach the choices involved in finding a solution becomes more immediate as opposed to a security professional who learns of a security breach at a competitor's firm. In the first instance, a less than optimal solution may suffice in the face of a need to take action today as opposed to seeking a more robust solution months removed from the incident.

Now imagine the magnitude of the choices made in your organization by each of your employees every day. The quality of each of these decisions has a real impact to the firm whether these impacts are quantified or not. Decisions made within each firm produce positive and negative outcomes, yet paradoxically, negative outcomes capture more attention due to loss aversion. Loss aversion posits that losses loom larger than comparative gains. Simply put: Organizational response to a massive loss of data or other failure typically results in major disruption and overspending to avoid repeating the event, with little attention given to the many successes in prevention.

Loss aversion leads individuals to underestimate losses and overestimate gains, leading to misleading expectations and overreaction to risks. Organizations that incorporate intertemporal choice techniques learn to develop a distribution of options with varying degrees of confidence over time. As these techniques mature with practice, risk taking and risk management improve, but can be accelerated with technology. The opportunity for improving positive outcomes and minimizing negative outcomes is the dual goal of applying cognitive and behavioral science concepts and technology to the management of risks.

Most firms take for granted that hiring the right people ensures optimal outcomes; however, the backstories covered here and historical evidence suggest that decision risk is the major cause of operational risks including fraud in the C-Suite. Given this evidence, security and risk managers should have a basic understanding of behavioral science and the possible impact cognitive risk plays in organizational performance and internal controls.

Cognitive security and the underlying science and research employed to explore these impacts is leading to new technologies for managing cybersecurity as well as a broad range of other risks. Security professionals should begin to familiarize themselves with these concepts to redesign their cybersecurity programs. There is evidence that a few forward-thinking security professionals are starting to make this leap, albeit in tactical ways solely to solve specific security problems, such as monitoring insiders or in the use of deception detection software. Technology vendors are responding in kind with emerging analytical solutions expected to grow over time. Smart systems have already proven effective in diverse industries such as retail, social media, healthcare, oil exploration, and financial services.

These same technologies can be used to simplify how risk is managed from an enterprise perspective from the cubicle to the board of directors. Solutions must be seamless, integrated, and directed at facilitating individual behavior toward the safe use of technology and the Internet. Strategic investment in training remains an important component for creating a culture of cyber compliance, but training must include cognitive risk concepts and cognitive security tools. In totality, cognitive risk management is the link to building trust in organizations through smart technology, enhanced decision making, and corporate governance infused with intelligence about its risks and opportunities for growth.

Decision support technology is also becoming a broadly accepted practice with measurable results in the C-suite. These tools are transitioning from marketing initiatives designed to improve customer engagement to new uses for handling more complicated problems in biotechnology, healthcare, investment advisory services, and even professional sports. Decision support systems assist the board and senior management in the development of strategic directives to address a range of initiatives important to the firm.

Cognitive risk management for cybersecurity incorporates human behavior into technology, raising situational awareness, enhancing compliance, facilitating decision making, and delivering offensive and defensive capabilities to address enterprise risks inclusive of cyber risks. In the interim, between the realization of advancements in security informatics and other smart systems, organizations must lay the groundwork for incorporating and managing in this new environment. Cognitive risk management is the bridge that prepares the path toward an enhanced cybersecurity program. Cognitive Security (CogSec) is one of many disciplines IT security, risk management, and compliance professionals must begin to understand and incorporate into a cognitive risk management program.

The findings in a 2015 CyberThreat Defense Report by the CyberEdge Group queried respondents from North America and Europe about their experience with cyberattacks and expenditures for 2016. Seventy percent of respondents are spending greater than 5% of their IT budgets on cybersecurity while 71% had experienced a successful cyberattack in 2014. Ironically, 52% of those impacted did not expect to be a victim in 2015. Counterintuitively, research evidence suggests that once a firm has been breached the likelihood of repeat breaches increases. European counterparts are spending in excess of 10% of IT budgets on cybersecurity with no apparent end in sight. The report found that, "Low security awareness among employees continues to be the *greatest inhibitor* to defending against cyber threats, followed closely by lack of security budget." The finding should be reframed from blaming employees and constrained budgets as negatives to an opportunity to rethink security strategy.

As expected, the challenge is described as a lack of resources and a doubling down on employee training, which is troubling given there is little evidence more of the same contributes to risk reduction. Organizations that ignore the diminished return of these responses inevitably repeat the same mistakes of the past. Organizations that develop cognitive risk solutions to reduce the burden (cognitive load) on employees improve compliance, with internal controls freeing the firm to leverage untapped employee engagement in more productive work. Compliance must become as intuitive as using a smartphone. Cognitive science can be as transformative in IT security as the "smart" phone has been to mobile phones.

Security professionals faced with the risk of uncertainty fail to change course even if the change is minimal. Changing defensive posture has its own set of risks. One is the fear of failure and how it would be perceived. The other is the risk of poor execution. Is there a middle ground? Yes, but change is hard even when there are better options, so let's first discuss how to make the transition and understand what prevents many of us from even considering a new direction.

The discomfort most people feel when faced with changing one's position, practice, or IT security orientation can be explained by a phenomenon called the endowment effect. Let me explain. Each of us places increased value on the things that we have incorporated into how we operate, what we own, and what we believe in. The best example is a house. As a house becomes a home filled with memories, experiences, and emotions, we endow it with increased value. When we decide to sell it we expect more for the home than we paid (ignoring market conditions), even more than we are willing to pay ourselves in certain conditions.

Expecting less than what we value in an endowment invokes loss aversion, which we have explained early as looming larger than comparable gains leading to status quo bias, explained as a strong tendency to remain at the status quo we have created in our endowment to remain at the same or better than our original position. Sounds confusing? Researchers have tested these effects to understand how these emotions impact our decision making. We all have seen these effects in others even if we do not recognize them in ourselves. The endowment effect is very powerful and helps explain why people hang onto their favorite sports teams, failed stock picks, and political positions even in the face of mounting evidence to the contrary in their beliefs year after year. We refuse to give up on the "sunk costs" in the endowed position, hoping things will change. Rational or not, these effects have real costs and prevent us from changing course when better alternatives come along. We must understand these effects and develop ways to recognize when they hinder our ability to make more rational decisions. Very possibly, there may be room for taking a low-risk approach using cognitive and technology solutions to enhance risk management in cybersecurity.

To decide which approach is best, security executives must develop a clear vision for what a cognitive-enhanced security program would look like at their firm. Establishing a list of benefits and opportunities for improvement is the first step. Conversely, defining the problem(s) requires an assessment of the key risk priorities for targeted enterprise solutions. Cognitive risk enhancements should address three key objectives: (1) enhanced risk intelligence capabilities; (2) an assessment of offensive and defensive strategies; and (3) the requirement that each solution reduce vulnerability at the human–machine intersection.

The assumption that the cyber risk challenge is related to a "lack of security budget" is not empirically proven. We now have independent data that point to an overinvestment in IT security with little improvement in threat protection. Striking the right balance requires a deeper analysis of inherent vulnerabilities, a "Lean approach" to cybersecurity, and a clear strategy that defines outcomes. The Lean approach assumes you, or machines, learn as you go and make corrections in-flight. In this way, there is no endpoint; instead a continuous assessment is conducted near real time, reducing gaps in awareness.

A Lean defensive posture does not mean that the current defense posture is entirely abandoned. The difference is that a Lean approach is treated as the R&D laboratory where prototypes are tested in spreadsheets or small-scale models before implementation. Trials are repeated until a sufficient level of confidence is developed in the outcomes. Data analysis is used to evaluate correlations and test assumptions; technology selection is informed by best fit to achieve the desired result. The first approach is used to validate the second.

By assuming a secondary Lean posture, security professionals can strategically simplify operations based on quantitative and qualitative measures. The goal is to anticipate a hacker's and/or user's behavior and systemically remove the clutter to focus on those programs that demonstrate best practice and revamp weaknesses. Adopting a Lean approach requires a shift in thinking about security and potentially new skills that may not exist in IT security. New expertise may be needed to think about how the Lean R&D laboratory might operate and how to unpack the variance in expected versus actual findings.

The point is the Lean approach is not a complete departure from today's "defend and respond" posture but serves as a complementary, proactive tool-set in current practice. Conceptually, the goal is to strip away clutter that reduces situational awareness. Data is used to drive security more effectively as opposed to adding security and hoping for the best.

The board of directors and senior management play a critical role in supporting a cognitive-enhanced security program. Board training on cognitive risk concepts is a critical first step in understanding its impact on governance. Senior management should also understand the very real concern security professionals experience when trying new approaches. Security and risk pros are reluctant to upset corporate culture; therefore, any change in security posture should be led by senior management and the board.

The board and senior management have the most influence in the three concepts that point to "resistance to change." We have reviewed these concepts already; but here it's important to review these concepts in light of their role in preventing governance blind spots and establishing enhanced insights into risks. The Endowment Effect, Loss Aversion, and Status Quo bias are as important as cultural norms in organizational behavior. The endowment effect is the concept that people ascribe greater value to the things they own when asked to choose between alternatives. Likewise, loss aversion is closely related to the endowment effect and was first proposed to explain the endowment effect. However, loss aversion refers to the fact that people have a tendency to strongly prefer avoiding a loss than acquiring a gain. You can see how the two are somewhat related in that as you ascribe greater value to something you own, the loss of ownership implies a loss that you would prefer to avoid. Status quo is embodied in a resistance to change and leads to a false sense of security. Change is inevitable but status quo bias is the false assumption in one approach to solve a problem or conclusions reached about the best course of action. Each of these concepts is self-limiting in cybersecurity and the reason we need tools to help connect the dots.

According to Kahneman and Tversky (1981), "Aside from values that influence his judgment, if the goods are not for immediate consumption, there is a time horizon uncertainty that is involved. The person has to judge at present time, what will be his future utility assigned to the good he is selling or buying. As the time period of judgment gets larger, the uncertainty gets more pronounced and the variance of the value distribution broadens. Even selling or buying an ordinary consumption or investment good might incorporate uncertain future value for the seller (or buyer)." Resolving these conflicts requires the full support of the board once everyone is in agreement on the path forward.

The uncertainty of changing strategies is one of the risks security professionals must weigh. Data and sound judgment must be used to overcome the emotions and fear of making a mistake on strategy. All investments in cybersecurity, whether effective or not, are sunk costs which, by definition, are costs that have been incurred and cannot be recovered. The Cyberthreat Defense Report mentioned previously is interesting in that almost 20% of respondents have no plans for change in their current posture even though the frequency of attacks has increased.* The "No Plans" cohorts may represent the approximate percentage of respondents who have yet to experience a cyberattack or are simply not aware of the presence of invaders.

Security has evolved in maturation around physical security, leaving huge gaps at the interface between human–machine interactions. Desktops, laptops, social media, and mobile devices represent the cognitive risk gaps in cybersecurity. Current cybersecurity posture implies that technology is the weak link when in reality the vulnerability lies much deeper in human decision making and the human–machine interaction as the root causes of gaps in security. To narrow the corridor of vulnerability, cognitive risk approaches should be used to limit exposure to attack.

Security professionals have only recently made investments in cognitive risk controls, the greatest contributor of exposure to firms. The old model of "defending the castle" continues to create a blind spot for security professionals with each additional dollar spent, making these investments more ineffective overall. Cognitive risk controls require a rethinking of security at the behavioral level for internal and external actors alike. As noted earlier, the greatest risk

---

* https://www.invincea.com/2016/03/cyberedge-group-2016-cyberthreat-defense -report/

and vulnerability lie at the intersection of people and technology. Anticipating the vulnerabilities inherent in human interactions on the web may require a reevaluation of convenience versus business criticality. As IT budgets increase, the dual goals of reducing the cost of risk while enhancing security are not mutually exclusive. Lastly, research confirms our previous suspicions about email, mobile devices, malware, and social media as leading portals to launch cyberattacks. "For the second consecutive year, mobile devices (smartphones and tablets) are perceived as IT security's weakest link, closely followed by social media applications," according to the Cyberthreat Defense Report.

The gap in cognitive defense strategies should not be a surprise. Risk professionals have not been trained in cognitive science nor had much exposure to decision science even though research has existed since the turn of the nineteenth century. Conventional risk strategies have developed along the lines of military command and control structure to develop situational awareness of battlefield threats. Employees need the right tools and training to defend the front lines on the cognitive cyber battlefield. Cybersecurity professionals must become grounded in applicable cognitive science methods and the emerging tools available to assist with developing more robust defense strategies.

The Cyberthreat Report does recognize a shift has already started, "security analytics, equipped with full-packet capture and analysis capabilities, is the top-rated network security technology planned for acquisition in 2015." Investments in monitoring and data capture are beneficial but do not represent remediation. The first step is awareness, which will be improved as security professionals learn more about the nature of these attacks, but the focus on incident data alone misses the core issue—the absence of cognitive risk controls at the enterprise level.

Research reports such as the Cyberthreat Report have become commonplace with a diverse offering separated by threat vector, volume, severity, and other factors. Cyber threat reports offer an interesting perspective on point in time events but are not predictive of future behavior and should not be used to forecast how security executives should respond in defensive strategy or technology investment. To make sense of the disparate cyber incident reports I have conducted a comprehensive review and found a number of conflicting factors that question the accuracy of the reports as well as the usefulness of using them to scope the dimensions of the cyber threat.

If you want to understand, say, for example, the total number of cyber incidents, cost of a cyber theft, the market size of cybercrime, or a range of other related questions you will find that the numbers just do not add up. Developing an accurate measure of cybercrime is much like calculating the size of the underground economy in every country. A great deal of estimation, guesswork, and extrapolation is used to come to reasonable assumptions. Cybercrime is even harder to measure than the underground economy in a number of ways. Like in the underground economy, victims of cybercrime are very reluctant to report these crimes or the extent of the loss and cost of remediation. Volume is a poor indicator of the threat. One hacker or a small team of hackers can launch an attack that impacts hundreds of thousands of events or multiple websites. The data do not isolate the numbers to a particular hacker or team of hackers, which would be more informative and indicative of the threat. Second, threat reports that calculate the cost of a cyberattack are misleading. The cost of an attack sheds no valuable information on the threat or the actual costs of mitigation nor correlates to the amount of technology investment needed to remediate the threat. Lastly, industry-wide cybersecurity research reports produce slightly better measures of cyber threats than vendor-specific data given the larger sample size and diversity of inputs to develop estimates of the risk. Cyber threat data are more art than science, as discovered in news reporting more recently.

What conclusions then can be drawn from various reporting trends on cyber risk? How should security professionals view the threat of cyber risk and form a basis for justifying a course of action in response to new threats? I suspect that the constant rise in cybersecurity spending is in large part influenced by the rapid rise in cyber incident reports, which tend to show a linear rise in cyber threats. However, the lack of credible data makes it extremely challenging for, say, insurance companies to create appropriate risk transfer strategies for cybersecurity. Data science is seldom as straightforward as threat reports indicate.

If the risk is overstated, the price of insurance is set at a premium and coverage is misaligned with the risk. If the risk is understated, the price of insurance is discounted and coverage is insufficient to address future losses. A similar anomaly exists in the pricing of cybersecurity stocks. In the early IPO market for cybersecurity, stock prices soared in anticipation of growth based on reports of ever increasing threats in cyberspace. Most recently, these stocks have lost value, with some below their initial IPO price, suggesting that the credibility of data to measure the value of cybersecurity stocks will rise or fall on company fundamentals, not threat data. It is not the scope of this book to develop a more refined analysis of the threat reports that exist. As before, I will use stories to demonstrate that security professionals should use some restraint in drawing conclusions from the data and instead should develop their own models for justifying risk transfer pricing schemes or making investments in new security tools. Let's now take a look at the risk of weighing the threat of cybersecurity by the numbers.

Bibliography

Al Mutawa, N., Al Awadhi, I., Baggili, I., and Marrington, A., "Forensic Artifacts of Facebook's Instant Messaging Service." In: Proceedings of the 2011 International Conference for Internet Technology and Secured Transactions (ICITST); 2011. pp. 771–776. Abu Dhabi, UAE.

Berns, G. S., Laibson, D., and Loewenstein, G., "Intertemporal choice—Toward an integrative framework," *Neuroeconomics*, Department of Psychiatry and Behavioral Sciences, Emory University School of Medicine, Atlanta, GA, https://dash.harvard.edu/bitstream/handle/1/4554332/Laibson _IntertemporalChoice.pdf.

Biba, K. J., "Integrity Considerations for Secure Computer Systems," MTR-3153, the Mitre Corporation, June 1975.

Brito, J., "ICANN vs. the World." *TIME*. December 30, 2010. Retrieved 2011-12-17.

Buchanan, L. and O'Connell, A., "A Brief History of Decision Making," *Harvard Business Review*, January 2006, https://hbr.org/2006/01/a-brief -history-of-decision-making.

Donaldson, G. and Lorsch, J. W., "Decision Making at the Top," *The Shaping of Strategic Direction* 1983. Basic Books: New York.

Farivar, C., "In Sudden Announcement, US to Give Up Control of DNS Root Zone," *Ars Technica*. March 14, 2014. Retrieved March 15, 2014.

Kahneman, D. and Lovallo, D., "Timid Choices and Bold Forecasts: A Cognitive Perspective on Risk-Taking," *Management Science* 39(1): 17–31, 1993.

Kahneman, D. and Tversky, A., "The Framing of Decisions and the Psychology of Choice," *Science, New Series*, January 30, 1981, 211, 4481, 453–458.

McLeod, S. A., "Cognitive Dissonance," 2014, https://en.wikipedia.org/wiki /Cognitive_dissonance.

Perlroth, N., "In a Global Market for Hacking Talent, Argentines Stand Out," *New York Times*, November 30, 2015, http://www.nytimes.com /2015/12/01/technology/in-a-global-market-for-hacking-talent-argentines -stand-out.html?_r=0.

Sasse, M. A. and Flechais, I., Usable Security: What is it? How do we get it? In: Lorrie Faith Cranor & Simson Garfinkel (Eds.), Security and Usability: Designing Secure Systems that People Can Use. 2005. pp. 13–30. O'Reilly Books.

Schwartz, B., Paradox of Choice, Harper Perennial 2004.

Shapira, Z., "Risk in Managerial Decision Making," Working Paper: Hebrew University School of Business Administration, 1986.

4

THE RISK OF WEIGHING THE
THREAT BY THE NUMBERS

In a 2015 *Fortune* magazine article, a pair of law partners lamented the lack of credible data associated with data breaches.* The law partners were attempting to quantify the cost of a data breach by looking through corporate 10-K filings of firms that had reported a loss of data due to a cyberattack and concluded that the actual losses resulting from a data breach were inconsequential.† In other words, the costs of a data breach were not significant enough for detailed reporting in the financial statements. Their findings: The cost of "a single stolen customer record costs probably somewhere between $0.58 and $201." The wide range in cost depended on which model one used to measure the cost of stolen customer records. "It's black magic," the partner told *Fortune*. "No one actually knows the costs."

One example of the challenges faced by data scientists to get reliable data on cyberattacks pointed to a report produced by Verizon titles "Data Breach Investigations Report." "Now in its [ninth] year, Verizon's report ventures for the first time to determine the cost of a stolen record—the amount of money a company loses for each pilfered payment, personal, or medical record. One of the questions we get a lot is, 'Do you have any impact information?' We've always had to say, 'Unfortunately we don't,'" said Marc Spitler, senior analyst and coauthor of the report, during a briefing call. He noted that producing a reliable estimate is no easy feat.

The reason, as Verizon data scientist Jay Jacobs later clarified when sitting down with *Fortune* at the RSA Conference April 20–24, 2015, is that whenever the company's forensics team would go back and ask companies about the financial impact, they would tell them that their

---

* http://fortune.com/2015/04/24/data-breach-cost-estimate-dispute/
† http://fortune.com/2015/03/27/how-much-do-data-breaches-actually-cost-big -companies-shockingly-little/

engagement was done. Sharing over. As a result, Verizon—and many others in the industry—have struggled to get quality follow-up data. Add to that the fact that the quantity of data isn't very good either, he noted. "It's not just bad data," he adds. "It's lack of data."

The cost per record model used by one leading researcher (The Ponemon Institute) is a straightforward calculation. There is more to it than compiling the data but the formula is rather simple. The sum of estimated losses is divided by total records lost, creating a linear formula of rising costs. As costs rise each year the cost per record increases as well. The approach creates wildly inaccurate estimates that underestimate the cost of small breaches while overestimating the cost of large breaches. Verizon, on the other hand, takes a different approach by partnering with NetDiligence®, a research company that uses cyber liability insurance claims to produce a cost per data breach number that is significantly lower than expected. Cyber liability insurance is relatively new and, as we discussed earlier, there is a lack of credible stochastic data for insurance companies to price these policies, which effectively lowers the cost of a breach.

Which approach is right or, more appropriately, less wrong? A very wide variance occurs between the two approaches owing to differences in how data are collected and the numbers crunched. For example, by using the straightforward cost per record model and Target's losses, 40 million payment card records were stolen at a cost of $200 per record, which results in an $8 billion loss, according to the *Fortune* article. On the contrary, when calculating the same breach by insurance claims Verizon's approach would have produced a loss of $20 million. A difference of $8 billion versus $20 million for the same breach suggests that security professionals should not make buying decisions based on these estimates alone! Target's costs after insurance claims paid were more like $100 million. Target is reported to have spent roughly $250 million in breach-related expenses. Both approaches are problematic in determining the true cost of a cyber breach; however, Ponemon wanted to clarify the differences in their online blog.

"By the same token, the couple hundred insurance claims analyzed by Verizon have caps, too. Since the NetDiligence data is based on insurance payouts—and since all insurance policies have limits (and sublimits and exclusions), it is highly likely that NetDiligence's numbers do not represent the full costs companies incur."* The apparent takeaway is that the business of developing cost of breach data is not without bias and/or conflict of interests. The differences and variance produced by the two results do not mean that either Ponemon or Verizon is doing anything wrong. Data scientists understand that all models have errors but some models can be extremely useful.

The point is not to determine which report (Ponemon or Verizon) is a better proxy; both have flaws that need further refinement, which both firms would undoubtedly agree is the case. The real point is that no one really knows the true cost of a cyber breach. More importantly, the cost of a breach in any generic scenario cannot be extrapolated to the cost of a breach in another firm with accuracy. The impact on any individual firm would vary widely by size and complexity as well as by the firm's response right before or soon after a breach notification is made public. In addition, the knock-on effects related to reputation risk, insurance costs, financial losses, audits, regulatory and law enforcement investigations, external consultants, and so forth are additional costs making the cost of a breach even harder to measure with much accuracy.

Even if these measures were accurate, it would not be prudent to apply a simple cost per record metric in developing a response to cyber threats in general. The best approach is to use one's own data to understand the risks inherent in your own firm as opposed to assuming the same patterns found in research reports apply to the risks in your business. Every firm has a different set of legacy risks; some known, but not yet addressed, and others unknown until a surprise failure happens in real time. Frequency and severity patterns will vary widely across firms within the same industry. This is the nature of technology risk, which presents challenges and opportunity for security teams to be more thoughtful about their own programs. The best way to lower the cost of a breach is to prevent or minimize one from happening in the first place.

As the frequency and severity of cyber breaches increase across the world, researchers have also attempted to project patterns of growth in cyber risk into future periods. These approaches are also misleading.

* http://www.ponemon.org/blog/a-few-challenges-in-calculating-total-cost-of-a
 -data-breach-using-insurance-claims-payment-data

What if the frequency of breaches declines but the severity of a breach increases? Conversely, if the nature of a breach changes, how would these be projected into the future? The bottom line is that increased spending has not resulted in risk reduction of the cyber threat. "According to a 2012 survey of technology managers in the US conducted by US research center the Ponemon Institute and Bloomberg, organizations that want to achieve the highest possible level of IT security—capable of repelling 95% of attacks—would have to boost spending from the current $5.3 billion (combined) to $46.6 billion, nearly a nine fold increase. Even to be able to stop just 84% of attacks, they would have to approximately double their investments."* As bad as that number might sound, Gartner, Inc., a technology research firm, estimated that worldwide spending on cybersecurity reached $71.1 billion in 2014 and was expected to grow to $76.9 billion in 2015. That's an annual compound growth rate of 95.17% over 4 years (2012–2015), right in line with the Ponemon projections given a margin of error.

Not everyone agrees that the money was well spent. Academics from around the world believe that money is being wasted. "How much *should* I spend on cybersecurity?" Professor Lawrence Gordon, a professor at the Robert H. Smith School of Business of the University of Maryland states, "it is important to remember that a 100% level of security is neither attainable nor particularly desirable, as it would not offer a good return on investment."* Professor Martin Loeb, also a professor at the Robert H. Smith School of Business of the University of Maryland, has created a 37% yardstick of security spend to data losses but these numbers are arbitrary and cannot be used in a uniform fashion within or across industries. Many firms have instead turned to the insurance markets for risk transfer solutions instead of working through a cost analysis. There are pros and cons with cyber risk insurance as well, in that each firm must consider their total of risk in the event of an attack that may not include retained risks not covered in a policy with caps on reimbursement.

Finding the right balance remains elusive because no reliable standards have proven effective. Getting to the right answer is also

---

* https://www.gfmag.com/magazine/may-2013/cover-growing-threat-the-untold
  -costs-of-cybersecurity-

influenced by behavioral factors. IT security is a balancing act of choosing between defensive and offensive investments influenced by personal preference, legacy system weakness, and other resource constraints. Most network architecture is the sum of short- and long-term decisions on infrastructure design inclusive of a history of partial solutions that grow over time to become tail risks to the enterprise. Tail risks are high-impact, low-frequency events that show up as unexpected failures. Albert Einstein is said to have described this phenomenon as "doing the same thing over and over again and expecting a different result." In other words, the cyber risk is hidden in plain sight but too often avoided in pursuit of other short-term gains!

Michael Chertoff, founder and executive director of the Chertoff Group and former Homeland Security Secretary, expressed very similar sentiments about a focus solely on defensive strategies.* "In an address to the Advanced Cyber Security Center (ACSC) Conference at the Federal Reserve Bank of Boston, Mr. Chertoff gave the keynote speech at the conference, titled 'Left of Boom: How and where to invest across the kill chain,'.... organizations that go it alone, and especially those that focus only on prevention to maintain their security from cyberattacks are 'doomed.'" Chertoff also warns about the inevitability of the Internet of Things (IoT) and new potential threats brought on by the connectivity of the Internet and devices.

With the Internet, "everything is connected by default," he said, "so things in your study can become part of the wider world. The camera in your PC can literally create Big Brother in your own room." Add to that everything from "Bring Your Own Device" (BYOD) in the workplace to apps that allow users to adjust the heat, lock the doors, and more in their homes, wearable medical devices, smart cars, critical infrastructure, and aviation, and it is clear that, as Chertoff put it, "you're not going to eliminate risk—this is about managing risk." Yes, the IoT sounds really cool and may add a bit of convenience but are the risks really justified? Connecting to the IoT is not inevitable; it's a choice. Connecting is a tradeoff between the "cool factor" and

---

* http://www.csoonline.com/article/2844133/data-protection/chertoff-cybersecurity -takes-teamwork.html

the risks of cyber threats. You get to decide to accept this risk beforehand or wait until security is sufficient. The IoT presents an appealing new target for hackers and opens up new vulnerabilities in the national infrastructure that had not been considered decades ago. Mr. Chertoff's message is a dire one to be sure, yet more is needed from stakeholders to change behavior toward risks in cyberspace.

Addressing the issue will require hard choices and tradeoffs between shareholders and stakeholders to balance security against the need to rush to market with the latest products and services. The only question is whether those choices will be made now or delayed again for the next shiny new thing.

Let's turn to a different topic where data may be more, if not as, important than tracking the cost of a breach. Most observers understand there is an extensive market for stolen data in the black markets for cybercrime but most don't understand how it operates or the extent to which it is self-sustaining. There is a dearth of research on the "Black Market" for cybercrime. What actually happens with all that stolen data? What is the size and scope of the black market compared to the cybersecurity industry? Thankfully, researchers are slowly piecing together details on the ecosystem of the cyber black market. The Rand Corporation has published a study on "Markets for Cybercrime Tools and Stolen Data." Authors Lillian Ablon, Martin C. Libicki, and Andrea A. Golay's "The Hacker's Bazaar," "describes the fundamental characteristics of these markets and how they have grown into their current state in order to give insight into how their existence can harm the information security environment."*

"The Hacker's Bazaar" is a look into the dark side of the web, with market forces resembling the sophistication and organization of major corporations. The evolution of cybercrime is mature and thriving, operated by savvy players who survive through innovation, stealth, and decades of new product development expertise. "The Hacker's Bazaar" highlights how the cyber black market has grown from a small ad hoc set of individuals driven by a motivation to prove their skills through notoriety and bragging rights into a complex and organized black market of professionals for financial gain. The black market is characterized as segmented, diverse, geographically dispersed,

---

* http://www.rand.org/pubs/research_reports/RR610.html

professionally organized, and mostly cloaked by sophisticated encryption for anonymity.

Like most market economies, the cyber market has evolved. Products are more sophisticated and specialized with a variety of goods and services available; communication channels are discrete and built around trusted relationships, and supported by a highly organized structure between groups and through forums to share and exchange information in a hierarchy based on roles and responsibility. Goods and services offered have grown rapidly in volume and customization from stolen records and exploit kits designed for bespoke stolen goods to intellectual property and information on zero-day vulnerabilities. The flow of products and services is facilitated by basic rules of engagement where "customers" place orders that are filled and scam artists are driven out of the black market by word of mouth. Price clearing markets ebb and flow with each stolen good based on market demand as well as the availability of the tools for executing certain attacks.

Access to participate in the black market is tightly controlled to avoid law enforcement; however, any voids left by arrested or disrupted players is quickly filled to grab market share. Law enforcement is improved and has targeted larger players but the cycle is endless, like in any organized crime operation such as the drug trade and mafia operations when those next in line quickly restore order after a kingpin is dispatched. A hierarchy exists, with the most skilled participants commanding the highest pay although a range of skill sets are active "for hire" or as a part of the cyberattack value chain. Cybercriminals have become more specialized and use automation as well as affiliates who are interchangeable as needed. As the cyber black market grows, new relationships are being formed to conduct increasingly more complex and diverse attacks with participants not previously known to collaborate. Underground networks are getting larger, with some estimated to include tens of thousands of people across a global footprint bringing in hundreds of millions of dollars.

The structure of the black market is expanding as well. eCommerce sites have been set up as "storefronts" and social media is used to communicate, share information, and offer "for hire" services and goods. Multiple skill levels are defined by the level of sophistication of attack and the "hardness" of the target, with individuals considered "soft" targets to "hard" targets generally categorized as organizations. (Target designations are based on the ability to steal data.) An active in-house R&D market has evolved for more targeted attacks aimed at specific systems, companies, or individuals provided by participants with the expertise to develop advanced tools. Market segmentation is increasingly becoming more specialized into "attackers," "product vendors," "stolen goods brokers," "services for-hire," cyptocurrency exchangers, and others who make up a population of participants generating a multibillion-dollar black market economy.

The exact size of participants and revenue is hard to pin down but it is expected to continue to grow with the advent of eCommerce and easy access to the tools to commit cyberattacks. Participants have become open in marketing "how-to" videos and guides on traditional social media sites to increase market share from the less sophisticated to increasingly more so as the next generation of hackers enter the market. This is a global marketplace today where early participants with great skill and training are believed to have started after the fall of the Berlin Wall as Eastern European economies contracted to include any country with open access to the Internet. Regions of the world are being divided and subdivided into areas of expertise and skill set dominated by Russia in terms of sophistication but parity will rise quickly as emerging markets mature in this market economy.

Cognitive security is a bridge but it will take time to develop against the backdrop of an adversary that doesn't stand still. A cognitive risk framework requires a large database for predictive inference and a broader perspective beyond artificial intelligence (AI) and machine learning with consideration for how humans interact with technology. A few examples of successful campaigns are accompanied by failures of equal acclaim. If you want to understand how Google and Facebook's AI search engines produce widely different results all you need to do is compare searches with a close friend. Without your knowledge, Google and Facebook have curated your results based on the frequency of your past history on their sites. You don't know what you are missing because there is no indication a machine chose what you should see. Anticipatory design is one type of algorithm used to produce results based on the interest you have shown in the past but it does not anticipate how your interests change over time. Anticipatory design serves up what AI "thinks" you want and effectively limits what you might learn in a more expansive search. The benefit of this approach is convenience but the downside is a reduction in exposure to content that may be potentially more insightful.

As the market has grown and become more connected the channels of communication have also evolved, with Tor diminishing in importance and new and more complex products resembling bulletin board style web forums, email, instant messaging, private chat rooms, private servicers and servers for-hire, and a variety of dark networks to improve anonymity and hide communications. The FBI has been very vocal in its warnings about these channels of communication and the ability of hackers and terrorists to use them to collaborate and carry out attacks but it does not appear that any one channel can be targeted with sustainable success as new approaches develop to stay ahead of law enforcement.

The cyber black market paints a troubling picture for cybersecurity professionals in general but also adds color to the need for equally more effective tools and strategy. There is a good news/bad news story and an opportunity to learn more about these markets and the participants who comprise the dark economy. Summarizing the findings of "The Hacker's Bazaar" and its implications, the takeaways are the following. The black market is now a global community of organized crime with mercenary-like players of varying skill set. A characterization of any one type of adversary is meaningless in terms of defensive strategy. Data, or more specifically, the value of specific types of data, should determine defensive response and security protocols beyond basic IT standards and compliance controls. A hierarchy of data protection strategies may be more effective than a layering of security. Nation-state attacks can be carried out with unaffiliated proxies who can't be traced back to a country or specific actor, making attribution more a guessing game of circumstantial evidence based on the intent of the breach or stolen data. Finally, data intelligence must become a part of the offensive and defensive strategies employed to gain insights into the behavior of participants in the black market to help anticipate future defense strategy.

It is important to point out that "The Hacker's Bazaar" is not a definitive or predictive narrative of the cyber black market. Much of the reporting found in the document is based on interviews that cannot be independently verified but is cross-referenced with other research to provide a descriptive impression of the players, structure, market mechanics, and the growing threat and sophisticated tools used to conduct these attacks. In addition, "The Hacker's Bazaar" was published in 2014 and covered events dating back several years; therefore, the nature and descriptions may not fully reflect changes in the black market today. Nevertheless, if the trends continue, this market will get bigger and more complex with new participants seeking to build a robust business in the dark economy.

Finally, the experts agreed on a few notable projections in the black markets that will present challenges for security executives in the near future: Use of darknets is expected to continue to expand as a means to develop and maintain anonymous relationships to grow these markets. Attack vectors will become even harder to detect through more sophisticated malware facilitated by encrypted communication channels and paid for with advanced cryptocurrencies. The collaborative nature of the black markets will continue to make attacks cheaper and faster than defensive strategies. Hyperconnectivity on the Internet will provide hackers with more targets to exploit and capability to leverage networked environments for a wider range of opportunities for attack. Social networks and mobile devices will continue to be prime targets of attack. Lastly, the market for "hackers for hire," "intermediaries, or brokers," and "as-a-services" providers will expand the depth and asymmetric of the black markets.

Cybercrime is not a monolith or one-dimensional but is instead a thriving economy of participants exchanging goods and services that are tested and guaranteed to produce a desired outcome. Further, the cyber black markets have created a virtual research and development process that is adaptive and responsive at a velocity unmatched in cybersecurity. "The Hacker's Bazaar" also helps to put into context why the cyber paradox is a persistent challenge that cannot be resolved with conventional methods of security. "Hard" and "soft" targets are vulnerable but clearly hackers prefer softer targets, which coincidentally are the least defended today in cybersecurity programs.

Imagine a scenario in which banks locked their doors with the keys intact and the combination to the safe taped to the door! Cognitive hacks may not be this simple but the analogy is applicable, as demonstrated by the growth in these targets. Unknowingly, users leave the keys in the front door for hackers by surfing social media sites and provide the combination to the safe by revealing administrative privileges. In many instances, this is accomplished just below the level of consciousness of users.

From a security perspective, the M&M defense (hard on the outside but soft in the middle) made it harder for cybercriminals to make direct attacks yet ironically lacks resilience to indirect asymmetric tactics. Cognitive hacks have exploded in execution through the use of semi-autonomous botnets with capabilities for testing zero-day vulnerabilities and launching email spam or distributed denial-of-service (DDoS) attacks. Individuals are the targets ("soft targets"), providing a much higher yield with the least defense against cognitive hacks. The news is not all bad and in fact there is evidence that a handful of firms are developing countermeasures and offensive tactics to strike back.[*]

In a 2013 attack, hackers commandeered 4 million Windows® computers with the Sefnit malware. The botnet connected via Tor, a dark web network, to communicate with its Israeli and Ukrainian masters. Microsoft became suspicious and contacted system developers of Tor with a question: "Is it possible a normal user using our installer would install Tor in the directory paths and as a service?" Microsoft was able to silently remove the malware clients from millions of computers but the attack was still alarming given it was the first time a botnet, as a collection of slave computers is called, used Tor in such a potentially powerful way.[†]

Tech firms have also demonstrated a preemptive strike capability using cloud-based analytics and global visualization. In partnership with the FBI, Microsoft "launched an assault on one of the world's biggest cybercrime rings, which stole more than $500 million from bank accounts over 18 months."[‡] The potential of big data is encouraging but the task is daunting against cybercriminals capable of creating an army of botnet drones aimed at attacking millions of individuals.

In 2014, security research firm Proofpoint "uncovered what is the first documented Internet of Things (IoT)-based cyberattack involving

---

[*] http://www.theguardian.com/world/2016/mar/29/microsoft-tay-tweets-anti semitic-racism

[†] http://www.dailydot.com/technology/tor-botnet-microsoft-malware-remove/

[‡] http://www.reuters.com/article/net-us-citadel-botnet-idUSBRE9541KO20130605

conventional household 'smart' appliances. A refrigerator was discovered among botnet of more than 100,000 Internet-connected devices that sent as many as 750,000 malicious emails over a two-week period between late December and early January. The refrigerator was responsible for more than 25 percent of the traffic but other devices such as 'smart' appliances were used in the coordinated attack. The number of such connected devices is expected to grow to more than four times the number of connected computers in the next few years according to media reports; proof of an IoT-based attack has significant security implications for device owners and Enterprise targets."*

The IoT gives hackers a wholly new and more powerful weapon to launch attacks by consumers who are unwitting accomplices with no means to detect or correct the security weakness built into these systems. Will the legal system prosecute consumers as the attackers barring no traceable culprit behind these attacks? Will class action suits include manufacturers, public accounting and consulting firms, technology vendors, and a host of other providers in the value chain? Market researcher, Gartner predicts that through 2018 over 50% of Internet of Things (IoT) device manufacturers will not be able to address threats from weak authentication practices and by 2020 more than 25% of enterprise attacks will involve IoT.[†] Market researcher, IDC has a different take on the threat of IoT. Regarding IoT, [Chris] Christiansen said some in the security industry already view IoT security as being a disaster. IDC, however, has a somewhat more nuanced view on the issue. "We view compliance and privacy as a significant risk that is even more significant than criminals and attackers," he said. Either way is troubling in that IoT exposes firms to additional vulnerabilities that did not exist before the introduction of smart devices.[‡]

Given what we know today, should changes in security be rethought for business assets? What would a more secure exchange between business and the public markets look like? Where should security begin and extend across the value chain of public and private communication channels given persistent threats? Many of these questions

---

* http://investors.proofpoint.com/releasedetail.cfm?ReleaseID=819799
† http://www.gartner.com/smarterwithgartner/top-10-security-predictions-2016/
‡ http://www.eweek.com/security/idc-analysts-identify-it-security-trends-at-rsa
  .html

should be debated more openly with the public to raise awareness and to get input on a range of unanswered questions before they become the cause of a major and/or national security event. It will always be easier and less costly to execute an attack than it will be to defend against one. Conversely, reasonable prevention must become intuitive, low cost, and less complex through less choice.

We are the creators of our own risks! Choice is a risk decision Internet users and developers of technology products must make more consciously. The equation is a simple one: More choice = More risk. Fewer choices = Less risk. Choice then becomes a spectrum of options in a cognitive risk framework implemented by the board of directors down. Directors of firms that promote, manufacture, advise, and implement IoT products and services must become more aware of these risks and take steps to ensure security measures are put in place or at least given as much attention as product features.

I call this "intentional security design" to describe systems engineering that assumes security breaches are possible and anticipates a range of limited responses to counter a breach. Examples include product recalls, system patches, and technology service agreements with providers to monitor for cyber activity and more. Similar approaches should be used in organizations as well. For example, on the one extreme, networked systems can be programmed to "guide" users interactively through security requirements with limits based on job classification. On the other extreme, a menu of privilege is granted by level of security.

Choice then is not an indication of personal trust as much as it is a risk management decision based on the value of the data. Far too often risk management and security is built on punitive repercussions producing limited deterrence against inaptitude or outright fraud. The goal is to reduce the need for technology users to remember a myriad of security and operational internal control rules; instead, the rules are preprogrammed into systems. These are not new concepts but are rarely used broadly in system architecture design.

As machine learning and AI becomes more common in network systems the ability to leverage prescriptive regulatory guidelines is an easy task for algorithms to handle, freeing employees to do work that adds value and reduces redundancy in supervisory controls and audit testing, risk management assessments, and other tasks that increase the marginal costs of security over time. The savings are difficult to calculate but one need look no further than the compound annual growth rate of risk, compliance, and audit costs over the last 10 years as a proxy with little to no corresponding decrease in operational risks.

Further, current risk programs are punitive in noncompliance, typically administered after a large loss or control failure, which is not only unproductive but also fails to provide substantive reductions in risk and leads to more costs. Punitive measures must be replaced with a reframing of enterprise risk through a cognitive risk prism that is intentional in design through technology and takes into account the human element and limits in cognition. The integration of cognitive security, machines, and humans is the next big challenge facing security professionals in the future. Progress probably won't be made in leaps and bounds as many expect; instead, advances will come in bursts of innovation and bumps along the way.

In wrapping up why there is risk in weighing the threat by the numbers there are a few considerations. Notwithstanding the outstanding efforts security research firms contribute to reporting on cyber risk, there is limited predictive value in the reports. "The Hacker's Bazaar" and similar research reports provide more color on the threat and nature of the cyber black markets and potential trends. Yesterday's attacks are not reflective of future threats; as the connectedness of networked devices expands hackers will gain more presence and increased opportunities to launch attacks with greater effect.

Security professionals are better served developing leading indicators with their own data to build internal talent and predictive powers over time. Research has shed light on a combination of offensive and defensive strategies needed in cybersecurity; however, until more comprehensive advances in machine learning and AI are available, firms should begin to incorporate cognitive risk processes to address the intersection of human–machine interactions. Security professionals shouldn't be lulled into a false sense of security. At a minimum, industry benchmarks and strong internal controls alone do not ensure deterrence.

One interesting development that contributes to growth in the cyber black market into a mature and active economy is a "confidence market," an implied and explicit level of trust in partners and tools tested under market conditions to execute increasingly more sophisticated attacks. Trust is a commodity that unifies participants in the cybermarkets; meanwhile, peers who violate that trust are quickly removed from these markets. Participants collaborate, develop, and share exploit tools, services, and expertise, leading to more innovation than possible alone.

Conversely, the market for cybersecurity products must also strive to restore trust in networked information systems with similar levels of defensive and offensive outcomes. A few considerations for developing a confidence market for cybersecurity are to improve security strategies, develop realistic legal considerations in cyber defense, and improve collaboration using scientific methods. Legal and governmental agencies cannot rely on nineteenth-century applications in cyberspace. One of many deterrents in reporting cyber incidents is the risk and fear of prosecution by courts and a legal system ill equipped to comprehend the complexity of cybercrime. How can regulators and the court system hold businesses accountable for a risk that the FBI cannot prevent?

There is a fundamental failure in modern institutions to understand the limits of risk management. These failures in risk awareness restrict the level of cooperation possible to combat an elusive adversary. Law-abiding organizations are not incented to report breaches of intellectual property for fear of blame and the inability to recoup proprietary property or even prosecute cybercriminals who carry out these attacks. The cybermarkets are compared to the illicit drug markets in scale yet law enforcement's response is to take out the "kingpins" to send a message. Drug prosecutions, like cyber ones, serve to drive participants deeper into hiding and create monopolies that are harder to take down, with players filling any gaps that materialize to capture market share. The drug trade and other organized crime syndications continue to thrive and so will a mature cyber black market until realistic preventative methods are developed.

A cybersecurity confidence market must "go dark" to cyber participants but be governed by "sunshine laws" that protect firms from certain kinds of prosecution and disclosure regimes that extend reporting to allow for a more thorough analysis of *after-action* events. A confidence market would enhance the protection of personal data after a breach with more secure methods than voluntary credit monitoring.

Victim protections would include a "safe period" of three to five years after an attack to deter or lower the value of stolen data. A safe period for victims of cybercrime would provide an exchange mechanism whereby personal data are linked with metadata that identifies it as stolen goods to devalue trading in black markets as a commodity of exchange. Methods for accelerating diminished returns for cyber-crime will require new encrypted eCommerce methods of payment, cryptocurrency exchanges, and advanced methods of authentication of personal data. In other words, traditional law enforcement meth-ods are less efficient in cyberspace to deter the business of cybercrime.

While many of these ideas may seem unlikely today, the idea of reimagining how government and industry responds to threats is common. The Federal Reserve has adopted new security designs in high-risk currency to hinder counterfeiters. Cargo shipping added armed guards in response to Somali piracy and bank secrecy laws were overhauled after the September 11th attacks as examples of a compre-hensive response to organized crime. Efforts by law enforcement must be supplemented with additional measures to raise the cost of crime and serve as a deterrent. Corporate espionage will require even more elaborate methods of deterrence; however, a robust confidence mar-ket has the potential for fostering innovation that cannot be achieved through singular efforts or waiting for a breakthrough from one quar-ter of technology. One could imagine collaborative design labs formed into "skunk work" projects funded by industry with subsidies from government that are then launched as private enterprises to allow the public markets to determine which ones survive. Competition in the markets would help foster better design while providing incen-tives to promote new cycles of innovation. However, this "utopian environment" is not possible without developing safeguards and trust among stakeholders. What is remarkable is how cyber black markets have formed similar methods without a central organizing authority or regulators to control the flow of goods and services. The lessons are hiding in plain sight, yet are ignored by not looking beyond the obvious.

As a final consideration, we are all familiar with the role govern-mental agencies play in the regulation of safety and health standards for many of the consumer goods and products we use daily. No fed-eral agency currently regulates minimum standards for the quality or security of technology products in use today. Technology is fast becoming a dominant product class that permeates many aspects of our personal and business lives while cybercrime, by the same token, is fast becoming one of the biggest threats to eCommerce and national security going forward. Ideally, the development of a self-regulatory organization devoted to tech security should be formed to govern and set standards for new products and services within industry for eCommerce. The formation of a self-regulatory organization would serve to broaden awareness of the importance of security and build confidence in tech products and services.

Absent a self-regulatory environment a governmental agency may require more explicit disclosures and warnings about security from technology providers if not outright minimum protections. Similar requirements currently exist for private contractors seeking work with government agencies and are a minimum standard demanded by some of the largest firms from technology vendors during requests for proposal. However, the vast majority of industry does not possess the same leverage to demand such vendors provide specific levels of security to accommodate their needs.

Examples of cooperation are growing in recognition of the need to form agreement on standards and processes going forward in cybersecurity. For example, nonprofit organizations such as the National Institute of Standards and Technology (NIST) are now widely accepted as a standards setter for IT including standards for assessment and authorization, risk assessment, risk management, and dynamic continuous monitoring practices.* In the long run, advances in cybersecurity will depend in large part on more cooperation and faster innovation. One interesting area generating a great deal of debate and controversy is the topic of "deception" as a cybersecurity for turning the tables on hackers. Let's take a look at the topic of deception and the debate for and against these tactics to turn the tables against cybercrime.†

---

* http://www.informationweek.com/government/cybersecurity/defense-department
  -adopts-nist-security-standards/d/d-id/1127706
† http://nvlpubs.nist.gov/nistpubs/Legacy/SP/nistspecialpublication800-30r1.pdf

5

DECEPTION

Hacking the Mind of the Hacker

"Warfare is the way of deception," said Sun Tzu, the ancient Chinese military strategist. The concepts of deception, counter-deception, and deception detection as a means of cyber defense have been saddled with baggage resulting from legal and moral issues for security professionals. Hackers, on the other hand, have become adroit in their use of deception as a means to achieve their intended goal to exploit vulnerabilities and improve stealth in the execution of cybercrime. Deception as a defense is not new, and like many themes from warfare, presents a potentially new arsenal of weapons available to counter cybercrime more effectively. So why has deception not captured the attention of security professionals and researchers more broadly? What are the benefits and limitations of deception techniques? And what approaches have proven effective in the field? Answering these questions requires a broad look at the tools of deception and the contradictions that must be overcome to build more robust defenses against hackers.

Deception, like money, is not for obvious reasons a topic openly discussed in public but this too is changing. This explains in part why there is still some mystery surrounding how broadly the technique is used today. Interest in the methods of cyber deception is growing broadly, as evidenced by the number of academic courses, technology vendors, and news articles on the various techniques available. The definition of cyber deception is not universal; however, a consensus is building. "Cyber deception is a deliberate and controlled act to conceal our networks, create uncertainty and confusion against the adversary's efforts to establish situational awareness, and to influence and misdirect adversary perceptions and decision processes. Defense through deception can potentially level the cyber battlefield by altering an enemy's perception of reality through delays and disinformation which can reveal attack methods and provide the attributions needed to identify the adversary's strategy."*

Other definitions include "Denial" as a companion tactic in combination with deception and other methods, making a succinct definition hard to pin down. In a red team/blue exercise by MITRE Corporation the term "D&D" is used to denote denial and deception techniques used in cyberwarfare. "Denial is the process of denying the adversary access to information, and deception is the process that creates misleading information through both facts and fictions" (Bennett and Waltz, 2007).

Miles A. McQueen and Wayne F. Boyer, researchers from the Idaho National Laboratory in Idaho Falls, Iowa documents the work of several researchers to form a deception taxonomy together with seven dimensions of system control to contextualize how various deception techniques are used to defend against specific attacks. More broadly, the deception framework used by McQueen and Boyer (2009)† may be used to thwart or mitigate the severity of an attack in the event defenses fail to prevent system compromise (Boyer and McQueen, 2007).

Deception consists of "dissimulation, hiding the real and through simulation showing the false." Dissimulation is accomplished through three techniques: masking, repackaging, and dazzling. Masking is a widely used method in security to hide data by making it unreadable or blend into the background undetectable by unauthorized users. Repackaging is used to hide the real by making the object appear to be something other than what it is or hiding its importance. Dazzling is used to hide the real by confusing the true nature or purpose of the object. Methods that induce confusion include randomization and obfuscation of identifying elements of the object.

There are three techniques used to create "simulation" described as displaying the false. The first of the three techniques is "inventing" the false perception that an object exists when it actually doesn't. Mimicking is the second technique used to invent the false by creating elements and characteristics of an object that does

---

* https://www.csiac.org/journal-article/cyber-deception/
† http://www4vip.inl.gov/icis/deception/deception-used-for-cyber-defense.pdf

exist in a decoy object with little value. The third technique for inventing the false is "decoying," which is used to attract attention away from the real objects in a network. A variety of tools are used in a deception defense strategy; however, dissimulation and simulation are the two core techniques used to hide the real and display the false. Deception techniques work best within a framework of a strong internal controls environment. The design of a robust deception program depends in large part on the level of maturity of security internal controls inclusive of its people and processes. Deception detection training programs are growing rapidly as security professions seek alternative ways to enhance defensive strategies.

The seven dimensions of security controls make up the Control System Cyber Security Framework. Each of the seven dimensions is defined in its ideal state representing a mature defensive posture with no gaps in execution. In recognition that perfection is not possible, at least not on a continuous basis, some vulnerability is inherent in even mature security programs.

The seven dimensions are *Security Group Knowledge*—subject matter experts (SMEs) of all network components; *Attack Group Knowledge*—the populations to potential attackers with the ability and interest in attacking the firm; *Access*—prevention of unauthorized entry by attackers; *Vulnerabilities*—any weakness or defect in the system that allows an attacker to gain privilege intended for an authorized user; *Damage Potential*—controls must be in place that prevent damage to the control system even when the network is compromised; *Detection*—alerts are in place and recognize any unauthorized activity in the network; and *Recovery*—the network can be restored to its uncompromised state immediately after an attack is discovered. Deception strategies are used in conjunction with each of the seven dimensions to make defensive posture more resilient than relying on subject matter experts alone.

A comprehensive Control System Cyber Security Framework incorporates applicable tools of deception in alignment with strategies to augment vulnerabilities in the seven security dimensions. Deception detection technologies include Honeypots, Honeynets, Honeytokens, Decoys, Threat Detection Canary, Deceptive Tar Traps, Misinformation, Misdirection, Deception Engagement Servers,

Deception Credentials, Emulation, Real Operating Systems, Frictionless (non-deployment and management), and Threat Intelligence.*

The technologies listed are not considered an exhaustive list nor do they represent custom-designed techniques learned through trial and error to prevent hackers from discovering new methods of surveillance. What the list does represent is the development of innovative approaches by security professionals and technology vendors in response to the asymmetry of cyber risks. Cognitive hacks as a security defense posture may not be widely in use but clearly the art and science of deception is advancing.

The benefits of a Cyber Deception and Autonomous Attack strategy seems obvious; nevertheless, lingering questions still persist around legal and ethical issues when using deception as a defensive strategy in cyberspace. The *Tallinn Manual on the Law of Cyber Warfare* (*Tallinn Manual*)† was published in 2013 to clarify the law on the offensive and defensive use of cyber capabilities in periods of armed conflict. The *Tallinn Manual* was a project undertaken by experts under the auspices of the North Atlantic Treaty Organization Cooperative Cyber Defense Centre of Excellence based in Tallinn, Estonia.

The project began in 2009, producing a manual on the law governing cyberwarfare. Among the many legal questions under debate were, "Deception operations in warfare are nothing new; some are lawful, and some are not, but does a person have to be deceived for an act that otherwise breaches article 37(1) to be perfidy? How does the law address the improper use of protective indicators and, indeed, espionage in the cyber context? And then we have the crunch question. If cyber deception operations become pervasive so that little or no reliance can be placed, say, on targeting data, what implications does this have for the ability of combatants to comply with distinction, discrimination, proportionality and precautions rules, and does that matter?"

The *Tallinn Manual* is basically a set of analogous international laws that currently exist in customary law but now apply to the rules of engagement in cyberwarfare. The language in the *Tallinn Manual* specifically targets cyberattacks between nation-states with a focus on

---

* http://www.networkworld.com/article/3019760/network-security/the-ins-and -outs-of-deception-for-cyber-security.html
† https://ccdcoe.org/tallinn_manual.html

the platforms of cyberwar. According to Myrna Azzopardi, author of *The Tallinn Manual on the International Law Applicable to Cyber Warfare: A Brief Introduction on Its Treatment of Jus Ad Bellum Norms*, "The *Tallinn Manual* deals with attacks between cyber platforms, even if repercussions are felt in the physical world." In 2007, Estonia was subjected to a massive and persistent distributed denial-of-service (DDoS) attack by Russian citizens and, by some accounts, traced back to state-owned organizations in Russia angry over a disputed war memorial. The firestorm that followed is the basis for the *Tallinn Manual*'s existence. Of particular concern are the rules of armed conflict or international law (*jus in bello*) and the rules to be consulted before engaging in war (*jus ad bellum*).

The application of international laws under the *Tallinn Manual* makes clear that "no single state has jurisdiction over cyberspace and a state has control over only its own cyber infrastructure and activities within its sovereign territory." Further, participants with "cyber infrastructure who are part of the global network does not imply a waiver of a State's sovereignty." Responsibility for state-run cyber operations are subject to international laws based on a set of rules and evidence of attribution, the first of which is "effective control."

Effective control is determined by the actions of nonstate actors who are determined to have "complete dependence" on the state. The second test is "overall control," which is less stringent but requires evidence that the state has issued specific instructions or directed or controlled a particular operation. One can imagine many a varied set of scenarios in which states in their conduct and actions may appear to come close to or cross over these boundaries, setting off rounds of debate regarding these behaviors. The *Tallinn* framework now provides a basis to test and debate the "bright lines and not so bright lines" of violation. As stated earlier, the *Tallinn Manual* does not draft new laws but bridges existing international laws to actions in cyberwarfare, but how does international law address the legal and ethical dilemmas in nonstate actors not covered in *Tallinn?**

The *Tallinn Manual* makes clear its jurisdictional boundaries, leaving each state to manage law enforcement and cyber incident reporting. The United States has set up a complex structure of state, local, tribal,

---

* https://www.fbi.gov/about-us/investigate/cyber

and territorial (SLTT) law enforcement partnerships, each serving as possible entry points for reporting incidents related to cyberattacks. "Voluntary sharing of incident information between state, local, tribal, and territorial (SLTT) law enforcement and the federal government is important to ensuring a safe and secure cyberspace. This document [website] details different ways SLTT law enforcement partners can report suspected or confirmed cyber incidents to the federal government. No matter which 'door' SLTT law enforcement uses, information is shared within the federal government to provide an appropriate response while protecting citizens' privacy and civil liberties under the law," according to the FBI's website.*

The SLTT partners represent a cohort of federal organizations led by the U.S. Department of Homeland Security and the Department of Justice. These organizations serve as the key points of contact for reporting each type of cyber incident or occurrence. For example, cyber incidents related to critical infrastructure are reported to the National Cybersecurity and Communications Integration Center (NCCIC); cybercrime or hacking, including financial fraud and network intrusion, is reported to the Secret Service Field Offices and/or the Electronic Crime Task Forces (ECTFs); cyber-based domestic or cross-border crime, including child exploitation, money laundering, smuggling, and violations of intellectual property rights are reported to Immigration and Customs Enforcement Homeland Security Investigations (ICE HSI); and cybercrime, including computer intrusions or attacks, fraud, intellectual property theft, identity theft, theft of trade secrets, criminal hacking, terrorist activity, espionage, sabotage, or other foreign intelligence activity is reported to the FBI.

The matrix for reporting cyber incidents is straightforward but no doubt requires a great deal of logistical support and coordination as well as vetting across multiple agencies. The reporting matrix also represents the scope and complexity of the cyber threat executed against organizations and infrastructure in the country. The impact on SLTT partners has resulted in a massive overhaul adjusting to the new roles being played out across these organizations.† In 2007,

---

* https://www.dhs.gov/sites/default/files/publications/Law%20Enforcement%20
Cyber%20Incident%20Reporting.pdf
† http://www.csg.org/knowledgecenter/docs/Misc0504Terrorism.pdf

a Government Accountability Office (GAO) report to Congress titled, "CYBERCRIME, Public and Private Entities Face Challenges in Addressing Cyber Threats," officials noted "continued concern about the threat that our adversaries, including nation-states and terrorists, pose to the our national security."*

The challenges in the report point to the threat by nation-states and terrorists to conduct a coordinated cyberattack to seriously disrupt key infrastructure; the lack of accurate data on the precise impacts of the losses incurred in cybercrime; the coordination of responsibility among numerous public and private entities for reporting, detecting, investigating, and prosecuting cybercrime; and the assumption of new roles by the Departments of Justice, Homeland Security, and Defense and the Federal Trade Commission along with state and local law enforcement. Those challenges have only grown more complex, as noted in the maturation of the cyber black markets since the report was produced in 2007.†

The learning curve for SLTT partners has been incredibly steep, as demonstrated by improved situational awareness in the scope and magnitude of the task to address even basic cybersecurity at the operational level. "In 2013, components of DHS's National Protection and Programs Directorate (NPPD) conducted a joint assessment of the physical security and cybersecurity of a federal facility. Significant work remains."† According to the GAO report "Federal Facility Cybersecurity: DHS and GSA Should Address Cyber Risk to Building and Access Control Systems," the Department of Homeland security lacks a strategy that (1) defines the problem, (2) identifies the roles and responsibilities, (3) analyzes the resources needed, and (4) identifies a methodology for assessing this cyber risk.‡

Further, "The Interagency Security Committee (ISC), which is housed within DHS and is responsible for developing physical security standards for nonmilitary federal facilities, has not incorporated cyber threats to building and access control systems in its *Design-Basis Threat* report that identifies numerous undesirable events." Complexity creates opportunity; moreover, the sheer size of the federal government

* http://www.gao.gov/new.items/d07705.pdf
† http://www.gao.gov/assets/670/667512.pdf
‡ http://www.gao.gov/products/GAO-15-6

and scope of services represent a target rich environment of vulnerabilities through legacy systems and a phalanx of security contractors
each interfacing across the agency landscape.

Under existing circumstances, network remediation is the per-
sonification of the cyber paradox, creating a zero-sum game without a new vision for how government should work. In a nonscientific
survey by International Information System Security Certification
Consortium Inc. and KPMG of 54 "federal senior managers or
contractors with cybersecurity responsibility in government," 59%
stated that their agency struggles to understand how cyberattackers
breached their systems; approximately 25% said their agency made
no changes in response to last year's [2015] breach at the Office of
Personnel Management; and 40% stated that they don't know where
their key cyber assets are located.*

The data in a survey of this size is subjective and is neither statistically valid nor representative of a systemic weakness across federal
agencies. Anecdotally, the findings may represent an opportunity for
a broader look at the overall posture of security, and deception detection strategies may be used to deliver better intelligence to security
professionals in general and specifically across the expanse of federal
government to improve situational awareness.

Fundamentally, government and business must begin to rethink
how business is conducted on the Internet and at each intersection of
the human–machine interface. Business as usual is no longer acceptable as the marginal cost of cyber risk accelerates. One often cited
example of the marginal cost of cyber risk is the impact of cyber espionage and the theft of intellectual property.

On April 15, 2011, Adam Segal, an Ira A. Lipman Senior Fellow
for Counterterrorism and National Security Council on Foreign
Relations, presented testimony before the House Foreign Affairs
Subcommittee on Oversight and Investigations on cyber espionage by
Chinese firms, and by implication, state-run organizations in China.†

Mr. Segal's testimony detailed Chinese state plans for developing technology through strategic cyber espionage. "Chinese cyber

---

* http://www.bloomberg.com/news/articles/2016-05-19/u-s-can-t-detect-when-cyber
  -attacks-are-under-way-survey-finds
† http://archives.republicans.foreignaffairs.house.gov/112/Seg041511.pdf

espionage has to be understood within the context of China's desire to reduce its dependence on the West for advanced technologies, and on the United States and Japan in particular. This goal is laid out in the 2006 National Medium- and Long-Term Plan for the Development of Science and Technology (MLP) which introduced the need for "indigenous innovation" (*zizhu chuangxin*) to lessen the "degree of dependence on technology from other countries to 30 percent or less" (down from 50 percent today, as measured by the spending on technology imports as a share of the sum of domestic R&D funding plus technology imports). China's vast markets and prodigious growth potential have long served as bait luring major corporations to invest in partnerships even though actual results have been spotty.

Cyber espionage is difficult to verify and even harder to trace directly to nation-states. "Since January 2010, Google, Nasdaq, DuPont, Johnson & Johnson, General Electric, RSA, and at least a dozen others have had proprietary information stolen by hackers, although how many of these attacks originated from China is uncertain. Attacks are becoming more sophisticated and increasingly rely on spear phishing (targeted attacks that rely on publicly available information) and other social engineering techniques"* which cannot be traced back to Chinese hackers. Accurate data on cyber espionage are hard to pin down owing to a general reluctance by American technology companies to report cyber espionage to federal agencies and the high cost to investigate in lieu of an inability to find and prosecute the culprits.

"Rule 66(a) of the *Tallinn Manual* makes it clear that cyber espionage and other forms of intelligence gathering directed at an adverse party to the conflict do not breach the law of armed conflict."† The *Tallinn Manual* defines "acts conducted secretly or secretively as 'clandestine,' whereas the term 'under false pretenses' refers to acts so conducted as to create the impression that the individual has the right to access the information concerned." In an interesting twist, a person who obtains information outside enemy-controlled territory is not engaged in espionage. Therefore, most acts of remotely undertaken information gathering are not considered espionage; conversely, close access cyber acts conducted within the enemy's zone of operation

---

* http://archives.republicans.foreignaffairs.house.gov/112/Seg041511.pdf
† https://ccdcoe.org/cycon/2013/proceedings/d2r1s7_boothby.pdf

using elements of espionage arc.* In other words, no matter what you call cyber espionage or how one defines the legal framework to limit it, the marginal cost of acts to gain intellectual property and intelligence will continue as long as the marginal gain outweighs the costs.

Whether the attacks emanate from one or more nation-state(s) or in cyber black markets matters less than improving techniques to detect and prevent theft in the first place. Cognitive hacks have become the most often cited cause for many of these incidents. Everyone agrees that human interaction, social engineering, social media, and email spam and phishing attacks create most of the exposure, yet paradoxically there is reluctance or an inability to minimize these risks through cognitive risk countermeasures. As the materiality of strategic relationships grows in the geopolitical sphere so do the risks. "Christine Wormuth, undersecretary of defense for policy, testified before the House Armed Services Committee on implications for aspects of the department's Asia-Pacific rebalance of losing military technological superiority."†

The past seven years have been a time of tremendous change and opportunity for the Asia-Pacific region, Wormuth told the panel. "As nations there rise and become more prosperous," she said, "it's created a lot of opportunity at the same time that dynamism in the region has created a much more complex security environment in which we are now operating." Wormuth points out that the gap in technological superiority between the United States and the rest of the developing world is shrinking and could close if America fails to innovate to ensure its leadership role in the world. As adversaries rely on asymmetric cyber strategies the United States must incorporate defensive and offensive strategies in combination with an understanding of the risks inherent in how humans interface with machines.

Cyber deception, also known as active defense, is one many emerging new technologies available for exploring more fully the development of a comprehensive cognitive risk framework for cyber defense. The Defense Advanced Research Projects Agency (DARPA) has been one of many initiatives active in developing a range of new tools

---

* http://www.cse.wustl.edu/~jain/cse571-14/ftp/cyber_espionage/
† http://www.defense.gov/News-Article-View/Article/604466

for cyber defense.* The DARPA Cyber Fast Track (CFT) program, unexpectedly cancelled in 2013, was expected to bring in cutting-edge cyber experts from a range of disciplines instead of the traditional defense contractors who normally participate in these projects.† DARPA funded a new type of cyber development program called "Active Defense Harbinger Distribution" (ADHD), a live environment for active cyber defense. DARPA's Cyber Fast Track (CFT) program was an experiment to shorten the process of grant funding used by the Agency to improve the government's ability to keep up with the speed of cybercrime. Interestingly, the project was headed up by Peiter Zatko, known by the handle, Mudge, who was a member of the L0pht hacking collective before joining the federal government as a grey hat hacker.

"Through the ADHD program many of the current active defensive projects are tied together under one common platform. It's free and anyone can download it. Using a live environment, cyber warriors can practice their trade by booting the ADHD on any Intel-based system from a DVD or USB flash drive, or run the test environment from a virtual machine."‡ Yet, there is a lingering disconnect among cyber experts on active defense. Some security experts would like to "hack back" or proactively go after hackers; others would like to make it harder for an attacker by introducing a little chaos into the process.

Still others are seeking a way to improve attribution or identity of the hackers and their intent. The ADHD program was designed to accommodate all three cyber defense developers in their efforts. The Linux-based environment is a stable operating system that will be supported without the need for constant upgrading to another version to patch security holes. However, the program was shut down because it was an experiment to see what good would come of an innovative approach to cyber defense.

Hackers have used deception successfully as a cognitive ploy to get around security defenses, making it essential to learn their "tricks of

---

* https://www.blackhat.com/us-14/training/active-defense-offensive-countermeasures
  -and-hacking-back.html
† https://ctovision.com/2013/03/darpas-cyber-tools-we-have-had-our-hands-on-darpas
  -distribution-platform-for-cyber-defense-tools/
‡ https://ctovision.com/darpas-cyber-tools-we-have-had-our-hands-on-darpas
  -distribution-platform-for-cyber-defense-tools/

the trade" and develop new strategies for counter-offenses. Hackers have learned that one of the best ways to avoid detection is to become a "moving target." In other words, attackers deploy a moving target defense strategy to initiate and sustain cyberattacks using stealth and the tricks of a chameleon to avoid detection. A moving target defense uses asymmetric uncertainty by changing the attack surface.

The Department of Homeland Security describes the moving target defense as "the concept of controlling change across multiple system dimensions in order to increase uncertainty and apparent complexity for attackers, reduce their window of opportunity and increase the costs of their probing and attack efforts."* A moving target defense is a version of game theory in which each opponent attempts to anticipate the moves of an adversary and uncertainty and change are introduced to keep the opponent off stride.

In a December 2011 strategic plan developed by the National Science and Technology Council for the Executive Office of the President of the United States titled "Trustworthy Cyberspace: Strategic Plan for the Federal Cybersecurity Research and Development Program" is a blueprint for the development of a new research and development program for cybersecurity. The Networking and Information Technology Research and Development (NITRD) Program is the Nation's primary source of federally funded work on advanced information technologies (IT) in computing, networking, and software.† The Cyberspace Policy Review's Strategic Plan "replaces the piecemeal approaches of the past with a set of coordinated research priorities whose promise is to 'change the game,' resulting in a trustworthy cyberspace. As called for in the policy review's mid-term action plan, this plan identifies opportunities to engage the private sector in activities for transitioning promising R&D into practice. In addition, and consistent with the PCAST recommendations, it prioritizes the development of a 'science of security' to derive first principles and the fundamental building blocks of security and trustworthiness."‡

---

* https://www.dhs.gov/science-and-technology/csd-mtd
† https://www.nitrd.gov/
‡ https://www.whitehouse.gov/sites/default/files/microsites/ostp/fed_cybersecurity
  _rd_strategic_plan_2011.pdf

The Strategic Plan operates around four main thrusts: Inducing Change, Developing Scientific Foundations, Maximizing Research Impact, and Accelerating Research to Practice. Inducing change is a new priority based on a Designed-In Security theme of custom-designed capabilities to build assurance against cyberattacks. In civilian terms, Inducing Change is the federal government's version of active defense strategies inclusive of deception detection and defense strategies, among other capabilities.

The federal government coordinates cybersecurity through a consortium of agencies through the NITRD Program under the leadership of the NITRD Cyber Security and Information Assurance Interagency Working Group (CSIA IWG), the principle group responsible for coordinating cybersecurity R&D activities. The CSIA IWG works alongside and assures execution of R&D initiatives through the White House Office of Science and Technology Policy (OSTP), the NITRD Senior Steering Group for Cybersecurity R&D, and the Special Cyber Operations Research and Engineering (SCORE) Interagency Working Group.

Simply put, moving target defense is part of the cutting edge framework for cybersecurity at the federal government level backed by science promoted through incentives and delivered through an environment of trusted platforms for delivery. Moving target defense, active defense, denial and deception, randomization, and deception defense are all members of the same family and conceptually make up offensive and defensive strategies to describe next-generation cybersecurity using asymmetric tactics to stymie hackers' attempts to exploit vulnerabilities in systems. Moving target defense is the federal government's attempt at becoming more agile while looking beyond traditional security contractors for the most innovative approaches to cybersecurity.

Organizations, whether large or small, must also develop a similar mindset. Research and development in cybersecurity represents an opportunity for new ideas and emerging technology but until we replace humans in the workforce there will always be vulnerabilities for exploitation. Technology vulnerabilities provide a target-rich environment for hackers, but even if we were able to find and patch every system vulnerability, there would remain a big gaping hole created by human behavior. Now that we have traced the digital footprint of cyber risk from the origins of the Internet to the halls of the Office of the President of the United States and the president's programs to advance cybersecurity innovation, it is now time to consider the weakest link—human behavior. What is a Cognitive Risk Framework for Cybersecurity?

References

Azzopardi, M., The Tallinn Manual on the International Law Applicable to Cyber Warfare: A Brief Introduction on Its Treatment of Jus Ad Bellum Norms (October 2, 2013). ELSA Malta Law Review, 3, 2013.

Bennett, M. and Waltz, E., *Counterdeception: Principles and Applications for National Security*, Artech, House, Boston, 2007, 335 pp.

Boyer, W. F. and McQueen, M. A., "Ideal Based Cyber Security Technical Metrics for Control Systems," CRITIS'07 2nd International Workshop on Critical Information Infrastructures Security, October 3–5, 2007.

Federal Facility Cybersecurity: DHS and GSA Should Address Cyber Risk to Building and Access Control Systems, GAO-15-6, Published: December 12, 2014. Publicly Released: January 12, 2015.

McQueen, M. A. and Boyer, W., *Deception Used for Cyber Defense of Control System*, Idaho National laboratory, Catania, Italy, 2009, 9 pp.

6

COGNITIVE RISK FRAMEWORK FOR CYBERSECURITY

Redesigning Risk Management and Internal Controls Design

Bounded Rationality: Executive Summary

Much has been written about the need to improve cybersecurity through increased spending on new cyber defense techniques and situational awareness, as well as offensive methods such as honeypots and advanced analytics for monitoring intrusions. Researchers have advocated that firms must increase spending to keep pace with cyber-criminals without providing any credible correlations for reductions in vulnerabilities as a result of these investments. Although there is a strong case to advocate for incremental approaches to improve a firm's defensive posture, the tactics and methods have not resolved a per-plexing problem called the "cyber paradox."

The cyber paradox is evident in the exponential growth of asym-metric cyberattacks in the face of billions of dollars of investments in cybersecurity defense and resources. One large Wall Street bank's CEO stated that he is spending more than $500 million on cyber-security. Given the vast empirical evidence that increased spending has done little to prevent cybercrime, now is the time for organiza-tions, public and private, to consider a more strategic approach. In fact, the marginal cost of spending on cybersecurity has resulted in a hidden tax on the national economy that threatens future economic growth and national security, as evidenced by data breaches by an alleged Russian hacker or hackers inserting themselves into American politics and in retaliation for Olympic sanctions.*,†

The Cognitive Risk Framework for Cybersecurity (CRFC) is an overarching risk framework that integrates technology and behavioral science to create novel approaches in internal controls design that act as countermeasures lowering the risk of cognitive hacks.‡ The framework has targeted cognitive hacks as a primary attack vector because of the high success rate of these attacks and the overall volume of cognitive hacks versus more conventional threats. "Cognitive hacking refers to a computer or information system attack that relies on changing human users' perceptions and corresponding behaviors in order to be successful," according to Cybenko et al. (2003). These attacks take many forms including phishing, social engineering, malvertisements, social media, fake news stories, and increasingly more advanced email spam attacks.

The concepts referenced in the CRFC are drawn from a large body of research in multidisciplinary topics. Cognitive risk management is a sister discipline of a parallel body of science called Cognitive Informatics Security or CogSec.§ It is also important to point out as the creator of the CRFC, the principles and practices prescribed herein are borrowed from cognitive informatics security, machine learning, artificial intelligence (AI), and behavioral and cognitive science, among just a few that are still evolving. There are no other cognitive risk frameworks to my knowledge that exist today for cybersecurity or enterprise risk management; however, it is anticipated that as advances in security informatics and cognitive science become more widespread even more sophisticated cognitive risk frameworks may be developed over time, including from this author.

In 1978, Herbert A. Simon was awarded the Sveriges Riksbank Prize in Economic Sciences in Memory of Alfred Nobel "for his pioneering research into the decision-making process within economic organizations." Simon's work was the first in a long line of scientific

---

* http://www.bloomberg.com/news/articles/2016-09-14/russia-says-there-s-no
  -proof-it-hacked-sports-stars-health-data
† http://www.bloomberg.com/politics/articles/2016-09-14/leaked-colin-powell
  -emails-show-loathing-for-trump
‡ http://www.ists.dartmouth.edu/library/301.pdf
§ http://www.pnnl.gov/cogInformatics/

study on decision theory, a branch of positive economic study with a focus on the theory of the firm. Gary S. Becker followed Simon with his work on "*human behavior and interactions including nonmarket behavior*" and most recently in 2002 Daniel Kahneman's expanded work "*for having integrated insights from psychological research into economic science, especially concerning human judgment and decision-making under uncertainty.*" New thinkers, such as Paul Slovic, among others, have made major contributions in framing the perception of risk as a discipline from which I will borrow in the shaping of the CRFC.

Why is it important to understand the basics of risk? Isn't risk fundamental and universal to the choices we make? The simple answer is yes; understanding risk has contributed to the long-term survival of mankind through trial and error and statistical analysis. Humans have learned to avoid those risks that are easy to comprehend or learned from the mistakes of others. However, there are risks we'd prefer to avoid through the pain of trial and error. Scientific methods have played a primary role in the discovery of breakthroughs in a variety of disciplines in medical research, space exploration, engineering, and more than can be listed here, but with a few notable exceptions these methods have not been widely used in the practice of cybersecurity or risk management broadly.

Financial service firms have led the way by employing physicists and computer scientists to develop specialized products and trading algorithms in attempts to gain competitive advantage in markets for a range of products. Surprisingly, the Black Scholes options model was the first of these strategies to make the transition from academia to widespread acceptance for managing risks in trading securities. Hedging and other risk management strategies are now in wide use but represent a very small percentage of the operational risks experienced by firms and are not reflected broadly in how risk is managed from the board down to the shop floor.

Likewise, the practice of risk management has evolved from a focus on internal controls and compliance to a value-based return by risk professionals. The hurdles to go beyond value to decision support are restricted by a lack of analytical skills across multiple disciplines needed to develop robust quantitative and qualitative strategies. Designers of risk frameworks have evolved in response to poor correlations in existing models and risk outcomes by adding enterprise and strategic components to existing frameworks in very broad strokes. More recently, however, risk frameworks for IT security, such as the National Institute of Standards and Technology (NIST) Cybersecurity Framework Version 1.0,* have begun to recognize the need to enhance and facilitate the human element of decision making.

One of the challenges to adopting a cognitive risk framework is the persistent lack of awareness about decision science and its concepts for understanding the role human behavior plays in dealing with uncertainty. Even though the science of risk management has created a robust body of research over the last 200+ years in fields as diverse as philosophy, medicine, physics, engineering, and financial services, the vast majority of risk management and IT security professionals have not been exposed. The advent of new technology and advances in powerful "analytics as a service" models will begin to lower barriers for building cognitive risk frameworks for a variety of risk taking endeavors.

Risk management is not as intuitive as we think; therefore, we are misled when challenged to make decisions with imperfect information. We tend to rely on heuristics (past experience and intuition) for decisions that should require scientific methods and analysis to fully understand certain risks that may occur less frequently or present as asymmetric anomalies. Cyberattacks fall into this category of risks. Fortunately, behavioral science provides guidance for developing a foundation for understanding how a CRFC can be beneficial in addressing a risk that operates below the surface of our consciousness. Let's first look at the subject of risk and why it's so hard to agree on a way forward in managing a range of issues using traditional risk management methods.

In the "Perception of Risk" (Slovic, 1987), studies found the judgment of how people evaluate risks to be much more complicated than first imagined.† How risks are perceived depends, in large part, on the level of sophistication one brings to the assessment of risk. Professional analysts use a variety of quantitative and qualitative skills

---

* https://www.nist.gov/news-events/news/2014/02/nist-releases-cybersecurity-framework-version-10

† http://www.rff.org/files/sharepoint/Documents/Events/Workshops%20and%20Conferences/Climate%20Change%20and%20Extreme%20Events/slovic%20extreme%20events%20final%20geneva.pdf

in the assessment of risks while the vast majority of us rely on intuition and judgment to determine what is risky. More often than not, the media, friends, relatives, and the frequency of tragic events in the media or the tone of political debates influence our "perceptions of risk."

Accordingly, communications about risk or risky events play an influential role in shaping opinions about what is or is not an acceptable risk. Slovic found that social groups or peers help to shape perceptions of risk avoidance or risk acceptance as a means of maintaining cohesion among group members. For example, the following two extremes demonstrate the point: *global warming and gun control.* Depending on which side of the debate you fall, no argument against your position is likely to change your view of the risks as long as you hold a view that is consistent with that of your group cohort. Douglas and Wildavsky (1982) assert that people, acting within social groups, downplay certain risks, and emphasize other risks as a means of maintaining and controlling the group.

The psychology of risk perception is complex. Empirical studies of probability assessment and decision making under uncertainty have discovered the use of mental strategies, or heuristics, to make sense of uncertainty in a world in which imperfect information fails to provide accurate solutions. Intuition and past experience may be found to be applicable under certain circumstances yet fail when the facts and circumstances differ in magnitude or there is an insufficient amount of data to develop an appropriate level of confidence.

When decisions fall outside of normal comfort zones or are beyond the scope of the aptitude of the decision makers, many simplify the problem in a process called "satisficing" to solve a complex problem with a more simple solution than what is needed to address the challenge fully.* Herbert Simon coined the term "satisficing," combining satisfy and suffice. By nature, we settle for "good enough," opting for whatever seems to expeditiously meet the minimum requirement needed to move us closer to achieving a given goal. We then stop looking for other ways, including the best way, to solve the problem. We rationalize that the optimal solution is too difficult, not worth the effort involved, or simply unnecessary. Expert and novice alike

---

* https://en.wikipedia.org/wiki/Satisficing

are prone to making these errors in judgment and can be influenced by fatigue, peers, or stressors that result in errors in judgment when viewed in hindsight.

Contrary to conventional wisdom, we are really bad at managing risks some of the time but we lack the ability to determine when we are more prone to mistakes of risk taking when faced with a novel experience or insufficient data. Further complications develop in our ability to discuss disagreements in our evaluation of risks when one party or both develop strong and/or diametrically opposed views of risk. "Research indicates that disagreements about risks should not be expected to evaporate in the presence of evidence (Slovic, 1987, p. 281)." Strongly held views are extremely difficult to change because they predetermine how information is interpreted in support of an argument for or against risk taking, leading some to an overestimate or underestimate of risks. When new evidence is presented it often is perceived to be reliable and informative only when it supports or confirms one's position or original views; conversely, contrary evidence is dismissed out of hand when it does not confirm a prior view. Bias in judgment often misleads rational thinkers and distorts decision making. These biases are formed over several years and become unconscious, requiring formal processes to avoid them under conditions of uncertainty. Perceptions of risk differ widely among individuals in practice and execution and are often influenced by factors related to one's background, social circles, experience, expertise, analytical skills, and other environmental circumstances.

Even more perplexing, parties in discussions who have no strong views nor take part in framing the problem but instead rely on others who do have a strong bias toward a certain outcome are thereby left to the devices of others and their preconceived conclusion about risks. Risk perception is malleable in the framing of risks and the influence of the presenter's communication skills. Therefore, one's definition of risk is in the eye of the beholder. When risk professionals are asked to define risk management, differences in definitions are often reflected as a diversity of perspective more so than the reality of analysis. Each person brings a different reference point in the shaping of his or her perceptions of risk. Directors may frame risks in terms of losses, stock price decline, regulatory fines, or failure to meet financial objectives. Security professionals may frame risks by metrics of remediation while risk professionals may focus on residual risks left unmitigated. These unaligned reference points muddle conversations about risk, preventing a coordinated approach to cybersecurity.

Paul Slovic's landmark analysis on risk perceptions sheds light on the process of making rational decisions. According to Sara Gorman, referring to Slovic's thesis in "The Pump Handle," "Early research on risk perception assumed that people assess risk in a rational manner, weighing information before making a decision. This approach assumes that providing people with more information will alter their perceptions of risk. Subsequent research has demonstrated that providing more information alone will not assuage people's irrational fears and sometimes outlandish ideas about what is truly risky." In Slovic's own words, "But risk analysis is a political enterprise as well as a scientific one, and public perception of risk also plays a role in risk analysis, bringing issues of values, process, power, and trust into the picture" (Slovic, 1999).

Perceptions of risk play a prominent role in the decisions people make. In one sense the differences in risk perception lie at the heart of disagreements about the best course of action between technical experts and members of the general public (Slovic, 1987), men versus women (Finucane et al., 2000; Flynn et al., 1994; Slovic and Weber, 2002), and people from different cultures (Weber and Milliman, 1997).

Slovic recognized the importance of understanding the impact of different perceptions of risk and the conflicts and disagreements that result. To deal with these challenges Slovak borrowed from researchers (Fischhoff et al., 1978; Slovic et al., 1984) who developed a "cognitive map" of risk attitudes and perceptions broadly to understand and predict expectations as well as responses to certain high-risk events. These tools have been used to assess levels of risk aversion or indifference in a tiered matrix by comparing the responses of the boards of directors, senior management, and the rank-and-file. The gaps in response between and among groups represent an opportunity to align risk perceptions, prioritize security efforts, and build effective communication campaigns. C. Starr (1969) developed a method for weighing technology risks to answer the question, "How safe is safe enough?" Starr hypothesized that humans working together will arrive at an "assumed optimum" level of tradeoffs between the benefits and risks associated with any activity undertaken over time.

Organizations rarely openly discuss these differences or even understand they exist until a major risk event forces these issues onto the table. Even then, the focus of the discussion quickly pivots to solving the problem with short-term solutions, leaving the underlying conflicts unresolved. Slovic et al. (2005) posited that "risk is perceived and acted on it two ways: *Risk as Feelings* refers to individuals' fast, instinctive, and intuitive reactions to danger. *Risk as Analysis* brings logic, reason, and scientific deliberation to bear on risk management." Assuming risk perceptions are binary; they are not zero-sum and balance the other out. These are simple conflicts or, said another way, different sides of the same issue. The trick is navigating the conflicts to improve risk taking.

Why spend so much time on risk perception? Risk analysis is a political as well as an analytical exercise requiring balance and input from participants across the enterprise. The most well-intentioned risk program can be sidelined through miscommunications or misunderstandings when negotiating different points of view on risk taking. Reconciling risk perceptions is more art than science but is crucial to building consensus and meeting expectations. A *cognitive map* serves as a catalyst for discussing the gaps in perception to begin the process of reconciliation. Slovic's cognitive map demonstrates how perceptions can be quantified and predictive of future risk responses.

The process of developing a risk response to high-risk events is helpful in reconciling the expectation of a "zero-risk" policy to the realities of uncertainty. Significant risk failures tend toward an overreaction to high-risk events. Instead, firms should expect and plan for certain planned and unplanned events and have a protocol for responding in kind. A. Wildavsky (1979) commented on this phenomenon,

> How extraordinary! The richest, longest lived, best protected, most resourceful civilization, with the highest degree of insight into its own technology, is on its way to becoming the most frightened. Is it our environment or ourselves that have changed? Would people like us have had this sort of concern in the past? ... Today, there are risks from numerous

small dams far exceeding those from nuclear reactors. Why is the one feared and the other not? Is it just that we used to the old or are some of us looking differently at the same sort of differences? (p. 280)

Slovic explained these overreactions to high-risk events further in his "accidents as signals" analysis of how a single event produces a "ripple effect" beyond the original event. A single high-risk event extends beyond the initial impact imposed on one organization in terms of costs (monetary or nonmonetary) to affect an entire industry and further leads to the imposition of excessive costs in new regulation to prevent recurrence regardless of the low probability or real systemic damage from the one event. "The challenge is to discover the characteristics associated with an event and the way that it is managed that can predict the breadth and seriousness of those impacts (Slovic, 1987, p. 283)."

A cognitive risk framework is fundamental to the integration of existing internal controls, risk management practice, cognitive security technology, and the people who are responsible for executing the program components that make up enterprise risk management. Cognitive risk fills the missing gap in today's cybersecurity program that fails to incorporate fully how to address the "softest target," the human mind.

A functioning cognitive risk framework for cybersecurity provides guidance for the development of a CogSec response that is three dimensional instead of a one-dimensional defensive posture. Further, cognitive risk requires an expanded taxonomy, or vocabulary, to level set expectations about risk management through scientific methods and improve communications about risks. A CRFC is an evolutionary step from intuition and educated guesses to a new way of thinking about the treatment of quantitative analysis and qualitative measurements of risk. A cognitive risk framework is more than a road map for developing measureable outcomes for cybersecurity and other risk practices; it is a set of processes designed to improve the information needed to make informed decisions. For decision makers to have confidence in a process for decision making there should be an explicit agreement on how to deal with uncertainty.

The first step in the transition to a CRFC is to develop an organizational cognitive map of strategic risks. Paul Slovic's research is a guide for starting the process to understand how decision makers across an organization perceive key risks to prioritize actionable steps for a range of events, large and small. A cognitive map is one of many tools risk professionals must use to fine-tune organizational risk appetite and expand discussions on risk while forming agreements for enhanced techniques in cybersecurity. The process of developing a cognitive map also provides an opportunity to evaluate the cost of responding. For some firms, the cost of response may have tangible and intangible benefits while other firms may decide to transfer or avoid certain risks altogether. Either way, cost consideration prevents sticker shock before an event and leads to more informed decisions about the appropriate risk response.

Some refer to this exercise as forming a "risk appetite," but again this term is vague and doesn't fully develop a full range of ways individuals experience risk. Researchers now recognize diverse views of risks are as relevant for the nonscientist who views risks subjectively as for the scientist who evaluates adverse events as the probability and consequences of risks. A deeper view into risk perceptions explains why there is little consensus on the role of risk management and dissatisfaction when expectations are not met.

For example, individuals who have experienced negative events of a significant impact tend to avoid risk taking while others who have enjoyed success from risk taking will be more inclined to take risks. Kahneman and Tversky called this response "loss aversion." "Numerous studies have shown that people feel losses more deeply than gains of the same value" (Kahneman and Tversky, 1979; Tversky and Kahneman, 1991). Losses have a powerful psychological impact that lingers long after the fact, coloring one's perception about risk taking.

Over time, these perceptions about risk and loss become embedded in the unconscious, and by virtue of the vagaries of memory the facts and circumstances fade. The natural bias to avoid loss leads us to a fallacy that assumes losses are avoidable if people simply make the right choices. This common view of risk awareness fails to account for uncertainty, the leading cause of surprise, when expectations are not met. This fallacy of perceived risk produces an under- or overestimation of the probability of success or failure. One of the goals of a cognitive risk framework is to make explicit that success and/or failure is based on the process of improving the basis for decision making and not a personal failure in expertise. Uncertainty, by definition, includes the possibility of success *and* failure in varying degrees; therefore it becomes important to devise ways to speed up the trial and error of learning using tools that help inform decision making. It also helps to inform the inflection point for risk response and remediation in the event uncertainty exceeds expectations.

A CRFC requires a clear understanding and agreement on the role of data management, risk and decision support analytics, parameters for dealing with uncertainty (imperfect information), and how technology is integrated to facilitate the expansion of what Herbert A. Simon called "bounded rationality." Building a CRFC does not eliminate risks; it develops a new kind of intelligence about risk.

Cognitive risk advances risk management in the same way economists deconstructed the "rational man" theory. The myth of "homo economicus" lingers in risk management much as it did in economics, damaging the credibility of the profession. "Homo economicus, *economic man*, is a concept in many economic theories portraying humans as consistently rational and narrowly self-interested who usually pursue their subjectively defined ends optimally."* These concepts have since been contrasted with Simon's bounded rationality, not to mention any number of financial market failures and unethical and fraudulent behavior that stands as evidence to the weakness in the argument. As the speed and complexity of business accelerates, cyber analysts and risk professionals need more advanced tools to evaluate the growing tsunami of disparate data points to better separate noise from insights into opportunities and risk. Let's take a closer look at what a cognitive risk framework for cybersecurity looks like and consider how to operationalize the program.

The Five Pillars of a Cognitive Risk Framework

The foundational base ("five pillars") for developing a cognitive risk framework for cybersecurity starts with Slovic's "Cognitive Map— Perceptions of Risk" and an orientation in Simon's "Bounded Rationality" and Kahneman and Tversky's "Prospect Theory—An

* https://en.wikipedia.org/wiki/Homo_economicus

Analysis of Decision Making Under Risk." In other words, a cognitive risk framework formally develops a structure for actualizing the two ways people fundamentally perceive adverse events: "risk as feelings" and "risk as analysis." Each of the five pillars (Figure 6.1) is a foundational building block for a more rigorous science-based approach to risk management.

The five pillars of CRFC expand the language of risk with concepts from behavioral science to build a bridge connecting decision science, technology, and risk management. The five pillars of CRFC establish a link and recognize the important work undertaken by the Committee of Sponsoring Organizations of the Treadway Commission (COSO) Enterprise Risk Framework for Internal Controls, ISO 31000 Risk Management Framework, NIST, and ISO/IEC 27001 Information Security standards, which make reference to the need for processes to deal with the human element. A cognitive risk framework should complement, not compete with, other frameworks as a common thread that links the human element of decision making with the imperfect art and science of risk management. The opportunity to extend the cognitive risk framework to other risk programs exists; however, the focus of this topic is directed

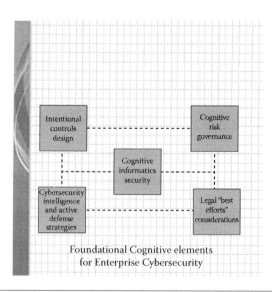

Figure 6.1   The five pillars of the Cognitive Risk Framework for Cybersecurity.

on cybersecurity and the program components needed to operationalize its execution.

The CRFC program components include these five pillars:

1. Intentional Controls Design
2. Cognitive Informatics Security (Security Informatics)
3. Cognitive Risk Governance
4. Cybersecurity Intelligence and Active Defense Strategies
5. Legal "Best Efforts" Considerations in Cyberspace

Intentional Controls Design

Intentional controls design recognizes the importance of trust in networked information systems by systematically engineering automation into internal controls design, reducing "cognitive load" for ensuring routine compliance and risk controls without human intervention. Intentional controls design is the process of embedding information security controls, active monitoring, audit reporting, risk management assessment, and operational policy and procedure controls into network information systems through user-guided graphical user interface application design and a robust data repository to enable machine learning, AI, and other currently available smart system methods.

Intentional controls design is an explicit choice made by information security analysts to reduce or remove reliance on human intervention for routine compliance and risk controls through the use of automated controls. Cognitive load refers to the total amount of mental effort being used in the working memory. Heavy cognitive load can have negative effects on task completion, and it is important to note that the experience of cognitive load is not the same in everyone (Sweller, 1988). The elderly, students, and children experience different, and more often higher, amounts of cognitive load.* Cognitive load can't easily be measured, with the implication that each of us will reach limits to our ability to focus over long periods of time in different intervals. The risk of cognitive load has been recognized in many industries yet is sometimes perceived as a weakness that must be overcome in others. The fallacy of ignoring cognitive load is, in

---

* https://en.wikipedia.org/wiki/Cognitive_load

part, a root cause of risk failures and helps explain how cyber threats can go undetected. No organization measures how much incremental cognitive load is added as each new initiative, policy, procedure, or sales goals is piled on top of a growing onslaught of information, data, and responsibility. Multitasking has become a badge of honor without consideration for the downside of cognitive load. It's no wonder humans are susceptible to cognitive hacks. Unconsciously, clicking on a spam email with malware is the weakness in internal controls exploited by cyber hackers. Cognitive load is a weakness in internal controls that deserves as much attention as systemic controls.

Automated controls must be animated through the use of machine learning, AI algorithms, and other automation based on regulatory guidance and internal policy. Intentional controls design is implemented on two levels of hierarchy: (1) *Enterprise level* intentional controls design anticipates that these controls are mandatory across the organization and can be changed or modified only by senior executive approval responsible for enterprise governance. (2) *Operational level* intentional controls design anticipates that each division or business unit may require unique control design to account for lines of business differences in regulatory mandates, risk profile, vendor relationships, and other aspects unique to these operations.

Operational-level intentional controls must align within enterprise-level limits and act as complementary controls to reduce gaps in vulnerability where humans interact with the network. The goal of intentional controls design is to limit discretion, reduce cognitive load, leverage efficiency, and enhance compliance through machine learning and other automated means.

The worst kept secret in many organizations is the lack of capital investment in back-office operational systems. Even those organizations that have made transformational change in the back office still require a great deal of manual processes and workarounds tying disparate systems together. The cycle of capital investments in technology rarely syncs up with the speed of business in an application economy. As budgets become increasingly constrained, the growth of regulatory and security requirements must compete for scarce resources, putting even more strain on security staff to balance competing priorities.

Internal controls are often external to system design, increasing workload on security professionals and individuals to maintain the status quo. Several industries have recognized these hidden risks and subsequent costs in cognitive load and have addressed them by making devices from cars to home appliances "smart." Product developers have come to recognize that we humans are busy, distracted, and frequently irrational when using their products; therefore security is being integrated into product design. I, for one, don't know how I lived without the rear-view camera in my car to parallel park.

The same approach would be adopted in a cognitive risk framework for network infrastructure with machine learning or AI used to execute many routine staff functions in internal controls, audit, compliance, and risk management. Intentional controls design automates the middle and back offices, allowing security professionals time to focus on situational awareness and higher-level risk controls.

Intentional controls design is about reducing cognitive load in security and operational functions. Cognitive load theory was developed out of the study of problem solving by John Sweller in the late 1980s. Sweller argued that instructional design could be used to reduce cognitive load in learners. Here is the basic problem: Modern industry has created a cognitive paradox of complexity unlike anything we have ever experienced before. As organizations compete for market share and respond to regulatory pressure, management responds in kind with new initiatives without reducing legacy infrastructure that adds undetected cognitive load on employees at every level of the organization. Worker "burn-out" is just one symptom and cost of cognitive load but also an opportunity to introduce cognitive responses to address a weakness that is largely ignored.

The cognitive paradox is reflected in diminished returns in technology designed to make our lives more efficient that has now reached a tipping point in effectiveness. Technology that requires active participation by humans has reached its peak in productivity gains and now is the major contributor to inefficiency and lost productivity. In addition, technology designers could not have anticipated the aggregated effect of cognitive load on any one individual. As the number of systems has grown in the 50-year history of the Internet, the need for multiple passwords, experience, and expertise with different operating systems, and the advent of mobile devices has peaked. Productivity growth is slowing as humans, overwhelmed by technology, information, data, and communications channels, represent the weak link in growth. We now need machines to accelerate the productivity gains humans provided in the late nineteenth and early twentieth centuries.

Early productivity gains were simply low-lying fruit that allowed humans to do more, travel faster, communicate easier, and work collaboratively in ways not possible before. Future productivity gains must be enabled through smart technology implemented through intentional design to facilitate decision making. Smart technology must be intuitive of human intent to increase throughput and designed to build trust when human cognition fails to recognize dangers in behavior. "Heavy cognitive load can have negative effects on task completion, and it is important to note that the experience of cognitive load is not the same in everyone," according to Sweller's cognitive load theory.

It is naïve to continue to expect individuals to learn and act on a plethora of policies and procedures without changes to the work environment to relieve cognitive load. The millennial generation is particularly susceptible to cognitive load at work as a result of mobile devices and the ways in which they interact with their peers and access entertainment using technology. Intentional controls design is the process of reducing cognitive load by incorporating policies, procedures, and efficiency into operating systems in the back, middle, and front offices.

Systems can be programmed to guide the user through the steps to complete compliance or default to standard compliance requirements without the knowledge of the user. In this way, the user simply executes the job at hand and leaves the details to the system. Over time, the machines learn to anticipate the best, most efficient ways to support their human counterparts through repetition of variations in how each person uses these systems, developing a best practice in real time aided by human input. Do you think this is science fiction? It's not! Google, Facebook, YouTube, and Netflix use predictive analytics that anticipates what you want before you ask based on what you have done in the past. Technology firms are using anticipatory design to reduce choice and make the decision-making process simple and easy. Intentional controls design requires cybersecurity analysts to think about making security controls as intuitive as using a smartphone or searching the Internet. Intentional controls design will occur over several cycles of software development but system analysts can prepare for these changes in anticipation of new technology becoming available in the near future. Choice is the enemy of cognitive load, leading to distractions and mental fatigue.

Ideally, the work environment must become easier to navigate in order for security professionals to make better choices and maintain situational awareness throughout the day. Choice, in this context, means decisions and the more decisions one must make to get an answer the harder it is to accomplish multiple tasks simultaneously and efficiently. Barry Schwartz described this phenomenon in his book, *The Paradox of Choice*. Schwartz further refined his work, describing the costs of choice, "As the number of choices people face keeps growing, negative aspects of having a multitude of options begin to appear. As the number of choices grows further, the negatives escalate until, ultimately, choice no longer liberates, but debilitates."* Considering the volume of responses needed to deal with cybersecurity, cognitive load may be highly correlated with mental fatigue and reduction in situational awareness.

One last point: intentional controls design must become a strategic objective of the board of directors and senior management. The board of directors and senior management should be active participants in the oversight of intentional controls design strategy. Intentional controls design also includes nontechnology choices such as policy on accessing the Internet at work, access to social media sites, the use of encryption, and other security concerns that leave a firm exposed to cyber risk. Hackers have become adroit at exploiting social media sites using cognitive hacks to get around hardened corporate cyber controls. Firms that have developed an explicit policy to allow millennials access to social media, advertisements infected with malware, and other sites leave a firm exposed by providing an end-run around cybersecurity controls. Qualitative and quantitative indicators of cognitive load need to be developed to help inform intentional controls design for systemic and nonsystemic controls such as soft controls that cannot be automated. Let's now turn our attention to the next pillar of the framework, Cognitive Security (Security Informatics).

---

* https://en.wikipedia.org/wiki/The_Paradox_of_Choice

Cognitive Informatics Security (Security Informatics)

Cognitive informatics security is a rapidly evolving discipline within cybersecurity and healthcare, with diverse branches of discipline making it difficult to come up with one definition. Think of cognitive security as an overarching strategy for cybersecurity executed through a variety of advanced computing methodologies.

"Cognitive computing has the ability to tap into and make sense of security data that has previously been dark to an organization's defenses, enabling security analysts to gain new insights and respond to threats with greater confidence at scale and speed. Cognitive systems are taught, not programmed, using the same types of unstructured information that security analysts rely on."* The *International Journal of Cognitive Informatics and Natural Intelligence* defines cognitive informatics as "a transdisciplinary enquiry of computer science, information sciences, cognitive science, and intelligence science that investigates the internal information processing mechanisms and processes of the brain and natural intelligence, as well as their engineering applications in cognitive computing. Cognitive computing is an emerging paradigm of intelligent computing methodologies and systems based on cognitive informatics that implements computational intelligence by autonomous inferences and perceptions mimicking the mechanisms of the brain."

The terms cognitive security and cognitive informatics are mistakenly used interchangeably however the two are different in practice and application so its important to distinguish the differences. Cognitive security is a scaled-down version of cognitive informatics that uses cognitive behavioral analysis, data science, and intrusion detection algorithms to detect patterns and deviations in network information systems. Cognitive informatics involves key application disciplines from two categories. "The first category of applications uses informatics and computing techniques to investigate problems of intelligence science, cognitive science, and knowledge science, such as abstract intelligence, memory, learning, and reasoning. The second category of applications includes the areas that use cognitive informatics theories to investigate problems in informatics, computing,

---

* https://securityintelligence.com/cognitive-security-helps-beat-the-bad-guys-at
  -unprecedented-scale-and-speed/

software engineering, knowledge engineering, and computational intelligence."* The distinguishing characteristics draw from developments among the different disciplines in cognitive informatics, many with much broader applications than cognitive security.

The difference between cognitive security and cognitive informatics also explains why many are confused about how soon machine learning and AI will be available in cybersecurity. It shouldn't be a surprise that technology vendors have already started to promote cognitive security platforms for cybersecurity. Cognitive systems are self-learning systems that use data mining, machine learning, natural language processing, and human–computer interaction. The tech industry has ramped up the hype and marketing campaigns in anticipation of promoting cognitive security platforms. Acquisitions are increasing in this space, with vendors offering solutions for devices to enterprise solutions. The problem, as usual, is allowing tech providers to define solutions before organizations have developed a plan to understand how these solutions fit into a framework for building an enhanced cyber defense program. Security executives should exercise caution and take the time to educate the board, senior executives, and the rank-and-file on the potential impact of a cognitive risk management program. Most importantly, security executives must understand that a cognitive risk program is not a tech solution; it is really a new way of thinking about how cyber intelligence and decision support enhance how an organization responds to cyber risks.

Intelligence and Security Informatics (ISI) is similar to cognitive security as a key pillar of a cognitive risk framework. ISI is defined as the development of advanced information technologies, systems, algorithms, and databases for international, national, and homeland security related applications, through an integrated technological, organizational, and policy-based approach (Chen and Xu, 2006). The definition of ISI should make it clear that a cognitive risk framework anticipates a comprehensive approach to cybersecurity and does not point to solutions that fail to fully address cyber risks. The asymmetry of cyber risk requires a more thoughtful approach to data, risk management, and cybersecurity.

The five pillars are designed as building blocks, each providing insights on cyber risks. The design of the framework should fit into a

---

* http://www.ucalgary.ca/icic/files/icic/2-IJCINI-4101-CI&CC.pdf

larger Enterprise Risk Management program for dealing with diverse risks facing organizations. With that said, the role of the board of directors is critical to the overall success and support of cybersecurity. The Cyber Risk Governance pillar puts into context how the decisions and behaviors of the board of directors and senior management contribute to defensive strategies.

Cyber Risk Governance

The Cyber Risk Governance pillar (CRG) is concerned with the role of the board of directors and senior management in strategic planning and executive sponsorship of cybersecurity. Boards of directors historically delegate risk and compliance reporting to the audit committee, although a few forward-thinking firms have appointed a senior risk executive who reports directly to the board of directors. To implement a Cognitive Risk Framework for Cybersecurity the entire board must participate in an orientation of the five pillars to set the stage and tone for the transformation required to incorporate cognition into a security program.

The framework represents a transformational change in risk management, cybersecurity defense, and an understanding of decision making under uncertainty. To date, traditional risk management has lacked scientific rigor through quantitative analysis and predictive science. The framework dispels myths about risk management while aligning the practice of security and risk management, using the best science and technology available today and in the future.

Transformational change from an old to a new framework requires leadership from the board and senior management that goes beyond the sponsorship of a few new initiatives. The framework represents a fundamentally new vision for what is possible in risk and security to address cybersecurity or enterprise risk management. Change is challenging for most organizations; however, the transformation required to move to a new level of cognition may be the hardest, but most effective, any firm will ever undertake. This is exactly why the board and senior management must understand the framing of decision making and the psychology of choice. Why, you may ask, must senior management understand what one does naturally and intuitively? The answer is that change is a choice and the process of decision making among a set of options is not as intuitive or simple as one thinks.

Simple examples include the choice to lose weight, buy flashy expensive cars over economical ones, or save more money for retirement versus spending on a luxury vacation each year. Choice becomes even more complicated in business, with multiple vendors vying for attention to their solution that is portrayed as comprehensive but narrowly addresses cybersecurity. The assumption that "if everyone else is doing it it must be right" is exactly why the board and senior management must think more deeply about how decisions are made throughout the firm.

Senior executives are expected to make a number of increasingly diverse decisions day in and day out. In many cases, these decisions are made with less than perfect information. Most of these decisions require little forethought; on the other hand, more complex risks such as cyber risk require new thinking. In addition, even minor risks have a tendency to build over time into a potential tail risk event when the right circumstances lead to an aggregation of risks. The tools one uses or chooses not to use to understand risks facing the firm will determine, in part, how successful a firm is at managing its risks. This does not imply that all decisions need to be run through a screen before a decision is made. However, management must have a framework for choosing among options that require deeper analysis. More importantly, the framework for decision making must also have criteria for evaluating acceptable levels of outcomes, including alternatives as new information becomes available.

Kahneman and Tversky (1979) point to situations in which perceptions of risk violate rational choice depending on how the problem is framed. According to Tversky and Kahneman, "we describe decision problems in which people systematically violate the requirements of consistency and coherence, and we trace these violations to the psychological principles that govern the perception of decision problems and the evaluation of options." Kahneman and Tversky describe the process of decision making in three parts: "the acts or options among which one must choose; the possible outcomes or consequences of these acts; and, the contingencies or conditional probabilities that relate outcomes to acts."

In many circumstances, the decision problem can be framed in a number of different ways using data or arguments to suit its framing. When faced with a choice(s) a decision maker adopts his or her own frame of reference in part based on group norms, experience, domain expertise, and heuristics (habits/intuition). The test is whether a decision maker is willing to change her or his mind when the problem is reframed but the facts and circumstances remain the same. Research has found that rational decision makers systematically fail this test when the problem is reframed. In other words, our preference for accepting or avoiding risks are influenced less by the risk but instead by how the risk is presented to the decision maker. Is this true in all cases? No, but it is more likely to be true in situations in which the decision maker has the least experience or understanding in dealing with certain risks.

The implications for the board and senior management are significant on many levels. For instance, investments in additional security measures or policies and procedures for cybersecurity should be evaluated based on an expected outcomes model that is testable, verifiable, and free of bias. In this way, a board learns to adopt better models for understanding their risk preferences for accepting or avoiding certain risks within degrees of uncertainty. Another way to say this is that decision making is the process of accepting or avoiding risk based on a distribution of probabilities of success or failure. As senior management becomes more astute in developing various distribution models for decision making under uncertainty, boards will gain more assurance in their governance of cybersecurity and other enterprise risks.

Cognitive decision models are not intended to remove the responsibility of decision making from management. Cognitive risk concepts for the board and senior executives help frame the harder questions with limited bias and provide better tools to solve them. Many observers may ask how this is different from what boards are doing today. How does this approach produce better outcomes?

Senior executives and boards have been very successful at applying a number of strategies for decision making without cognitive models but often settle on suboptimal solutions when presented with imperfect information. Cognitive models are effective in shedding light on suboptimal choices, providing new insights on these problems. Boards will use these models to measure the marginal cost of security against expected outcomes to evaluate best efforts solutions in cybersecurity.

The fourth pillar, Cybersecurity Intelligence and Defense Strategies, will detail examples for putting these models into practice.

Boards need to understand that cognitive hacks are fundamentally different, requiring new strategies and better intelligence to respond effectively to asymmetric risk. Unlike qualitative risk assessments, a cognitive risk framework is multidisciplinary, providing the board with perspectives informed by technology, data science, and behavioral science and creating insights grounded by proven methodology. These methods extend beyond narrowly defined big data solutions to animate offensive and defensive solutions in cybersecurity.

Now that we have laid the groundwork for *why* there should be a CRG pillar let's explain *what* it is and *how* it works. Boards are inundated with advice from external auditors, advisers, the media, and regulators all demanding a response to one of the most complex risks facing an organization. It is clear that boards have been responsive to this threat with the authorization of billions of dollars in investment in security, staff, and external resources to address the risk. The problem is not a lack of commitment or intent to respond to cyber risk. Board awareness on cyber risk is high but has reached a level of frustration in terms of next steps. The frustration is evident in the cyber paradox, with spending growth rates far exceeding revenue-producing initiatives. In light of these new pressures, boards have responded appropriately to date using current benchmarks in best practice. Awareness of the problem is not enough in tackling a growing threat with diminished tools.

What is becoming clear in the evidence is that a multidisciplinary approach shows promise but existing technology is not enough to respond to cognitive hacks. Boards must also be aware of the risks associated with human–machine interactions to develop a range of responses including qualitative and quantitative strategies. Researchers have found the human–machine interaction one of the greatest vulnerabilities within an organization.* Poorly designed human–machine interfaces can lead to many unexpected problems. A classic example of this is the Three Mile Island accident, a nuclear meltdown accident, where investigations concluded that the design of the human–machine interface was at least partly responsible for the disaster.†

---

* https://en.wikipedia.org/wiki/Human%E2%80%93computer_interaction
† https://ergoweb.com/what-is-cognitive-ergonomics/

Vulnerability assessments must also expand beyond network security to include social media, email, mobile devices, and other communication channels as well as encryption technologies. Defensive strategies must continue to evolve to account for the asymmetry of cyber risk. Boards need solutions that evolve alongside cyber risks that are sustainable and mature as the business grows. The conclusion is that boards can no longer follow the crowd and expect a different result. A new path is needed to counter the asymmetry of cyber risk.

The CRG pillar should be formed as a separate oversight committee on the board independent from the audit committee depending on the size and complexity of the firm. The CRG committee is responsible for developing a long-term security strategy, evaluating new technology, and sponsoring research and development for new security approaches using a data-dependent approach. The CRG committee makes recommendations and develops awareness strategies to the board and senior management by advancing cybersecurity in support of the Cybersecurity Intelligence and Defense Strategies (CIDS) pillar. CIDS serves as the laboratory of cybersecurity while the CRG provides direction and monitors the outcomes of new strategies.

CRG committee representation should include a multidisciplinary team of diverse backgrounds who are well versed in the cognitive risk five pillars described earlier. The CRG committee should be tasked with maintaining relationships and collaborating with governmental agencies, law enforcement, as well as academia and cybersecurity entrepreneurs expert in nontraditional security. The mission of the CRG is to develop metrics-based outcomes for performance and sponsor research and innovation in cybersecurity. In other words, the CRG committee must be strategic in its focus, with the CIDS focused on testing, execution, reporting, and monitoring results to CRG members.

It is now time to describe the fourth pillar, Cybersecurity Intelligence and Defense Strategies.

Cybersecurity Intelligence and Defense Strategies

Information on its own may be of utility to the commander, but when related to other information about the operational environment and considered in the light of past experience, it gives rise to a new understanding of the information, which may be termed "intelligence."

The Cybersecurity Intelligence and Defense Strategies (CIDS) pillar is based on the principles of the 17-member Defense Intelligence and Intelligence community "Joint Intelligence" report. Cybersecurity intelligence is conducted to develop information on four levels: Strategic, Operational, Tactical, and Asymmetrical. *Strategic* intelligence should be developed for the board of directors, senior management, and the CRG committee. *Operational* intelligence should be designed to provide security professionals with an understanding of threats and operational environment vulnerabilities. *Tactical* intelligence must provide directional guidance for offensive and defensive security strategies. *Asymmetrical* intelligence strategies include monitoring the cyber black market and other market intelligence from law enforcement and other means as possible.

CIDS also acts as the laboratory for cybersecurity intelligence responsible for leading the human and technology security practice through a data-dependent format to provide rapid response capabilities. Information gathering is the process of providing organizational leadership with context for improved decision making for current and forward-looking objectives that are key to operational success or to avoid operational failure. Converting information into intelligence requires an organization to develop formal processes, capabilities, analysis, monitoring, and communication channels that enhance its ability to respond appropriately and in a timely manner. Intelligence gathering assumes that the organization has in place objectives for cybersecurity that are well defined through plans of execution and possesses capabilities to respond accordingly to countermeasures (surprise) as well as expected outcomes.

The principles of intelligence gathering include the following characteristics: *Perspective*—understand the operational environment; *Synchronization*—synchronize intelligence with plans and operations; *Integrity*—remain intellectually honest; *Unity of Effort*—cooperate to achieve a common objective; *Prioritization*—prioritize based on leadership guidance; *Excellence*—strive to achieve the highest standards of quality; *Prediction*—accept the risk of predicting adversary intentions; *Agility*—remain flexible and adapt to changing situations; and *Collaboration*—leverage expertise of diverse analytical resources.

Cyber risk intelligence is analogous to military operations in that the adversary is equally adept or more so at intelligence gathering, which requires countermeasures in intelligence gathering. In cyberspace, organizations must become aware on three critical fronts. The first two are one's own critical vulnerabilities and the presence of intelligence gathering strategies by the adversary as they occur. Mitigation of the former and response for the latter make up part of the offensive and defensive strategies informed by cyber intelligence. Finally, the third front involves evaluating the effectiveness of the response and completeness of mitigation efforts to deter future attacks. The difference between raw data/information and intelligence is "two critical features that distinguish it from information: Intelligence allows anticipation or prediction of future situations and circumstances, and it informs decisions by illuminating the differences in available courses of action (COAs)."* Data management, data science, and the processes associated with converting information into usable intelligence are equally important.

The CIDS will also evaluate the efficacy of new technology on a trial basis before implementing into production. New product intelligence is critical to maximizing the cost–benefit analysis of security assets but also ensures new products are effective in field tests. In some cases, the CIDS will evaluate emerging technologies or participate in joint studies to build operational expertise and learn diverse capabilities not yet in use broadly. Evaluation criteria will be developed jointly by the CRG and CIDS based partly on intelligence gathering but also in anticipation of emerging technologies for future installation. The third component of cyber intelligence involves cognitive risk assessments of human–machine interactions. The intelligence centers on how human behavior contributes to cyber risk and the formulation of strategies to strengthen security while making compliance more intuitive for the user. The three main thrusts of intelligence gathering are operational awareness, technological and cost-efficient offensive and defensive security applications, and finally, cognitive security solutions.

There is one additional consideration that requires a mention but is beyond the full scope of this work. The fourth consideration is "ethical

---

* http://www.dtic.mil/doctrine/new_pubs/jp2_0.pdf

dilemmas" in intelligence communications and reporting. A cognitive risk framework does not solve ethical challenges associated with intelligence gathering. Ethics and conflicts of interest must be clear and approved by the board of trustees. Independence is a critical component of the CIDS pillar and demonstrates why it should be separate from the audit committee and guided by mechanisms of checks and balances to ensure that intelligence is free of bias or political agenda.

Military annals have a history of examples of civilian leadership ignoring intelligence or deciding strategy based on incomplete analysis, resulting in tragic consequences. General Colin Powell, chairman of the Joint Chiefs of Staff from 1989 to 1993, gave the following advice to the Joint Staff J-2 on November 1992, "Tell me what you know... tell me what you don't know....tell me what you think....always distinguish which is which." Risk intelligence is most effective when verbal and written communications are clear. General Powell's point is clear; however, there are times when management may not like or agree with the data or the interpretation of the findings. Formal and informal processes must be put in place to reduce the potential for "interpretation shopping" to fit a narrative. To address this natural tendency to manage intelligence, the CRG and CIDS must report the data without bias or influence while allowing the board to make its own interpretation.

Any adjustments to the CRG and CIDS intelligence gathering process must be documented and signed off by the board and senior officers of the firm with justifications for the adjustments. According to the J-2 report, "Intelligence analysts should distinguish between what is known with confidence based on the facts of the situation and the operational environment (OE) and what are untested assumptions. Intelligence can be facts that have been observed, or it can be a conclusion based on facts of such certainty that it is considered to be knowledge. Intelligence can also be conclusions and estimates deduced from incomplete sets of facts or induced from potentially related facts. The commander's determination of appropriate objectives and operations may rest on knowing whether intelligence is 'fact' or 'assumption,' and knowing the particular logic used to develop an intelligence estimate, as well as knowing the confidence level the J-2 places on the provided intelligence and related analytic conclusions." Intelligence is a critical component of a CRFC to ensure senior management has a full picture of the threat from data external to its organization in context with data analytics inside the firm. A holistic intelligence process is needed to identify trends not yet evident from internal data.

Finally, I would like to turn to a final pillar that takes into account an event that leads to a cyber breach even with the best efforts of any organization. The fifth pillar is Legal "Best Efforts" Considerations in Cyberspace.

Legal "Best Efforts" Considerations in Cyberspace

To say that the legal community is struggling with how to address cyber risks is an understatement: on the one hand, addressing the protection of their own clients' data and, on the other hand, determining negligence in a global environment where no organization can ensure against a data breach with 100% certainty. "The ABA [American Bar Association] Cybersecurity Legal Task Force, chaired by Judy Miller and Harvey Rishikof, is hard at work on the *Cyber and Data Security Handbook*. The *ABA Cybersecurity Handbook* offers practical cyber-threat information, guidance, and strategies for lawyers, law firm attorneys, in-house counsel, government attorneys, and public interest attorneys."[*] Law firms have the same challenges as all other organizations but also have a higher standard in their ethical rules that require confidentiality of attorney–client and work product data. I looked to the guidance provided by the ABA to frame the fifth pillar of the CRFC.

The concept of "best efforts" is a contractual term used to obligate the parties to make their best attempt to accomplish a goal, typically used when there is uncertainty about the ability to meet a goal. "Courts have not required that a party under a duty to use best efforts to accomplish a given goal make every available effort to do so, regardless of the harm to it. Some courts have held that the appropriate standard is one of good faith. *Black's Law Dictionary* 701 (7th ed. 1999) has defined good faith as 'A state of mind consisting in (1) honesty in belief or purpose, (2) faithfulness to one's duty or obligation, (3) observance of reasonable commercial standards of fair dealing in a given trade or business, or (4) absence of intent to defraud or to seek unconscionable advantage.'"[†]

---

[*] http://www.americanbar.org/publications/law_practice_magazine/2013/july-august/cybersecurity-law-firms.html
[†] http://thelawdictionary.org/best-efforts/

Boards of directors and senior executives are held to these standards by contractual agreement whether aware of these standards or not in the event a breach occurs. The ABA has adopted a security program guide by the Carnegie Mellon University's Software Engineering Institute. The Carnegie Mellon Enterprise Security Program (ESP) has been tailored for law firms as a prescriptive set of security-related activities as well as incident response and ethical considerations. The Carnegie Mellow ESP spells out "some basic activities must be undertaken to establish a security program, no matter which best practice a firm decides to follow. (Note that they are all harmonized and can be adjusted for small firms.) Technical staff will manage most of these activities, but firm partners and staff need to provide critical input. Firm management must define security roles and responsibilities, develop top-level policies, and exercise oversight. This means reviewing findings from critical activities; receiving regular reports on intrusions, system usage and compliance with policies and procedures; and reviewing the security plans and budget."

This information is not legal guidance to comply with an organization's best efforts requirements. The information is provided to bring awareness to the importance of the board and senior management's participation to ensure all bases are covered in cyber risk. The CRFC's fifth pillar completes the framework as a link to existing standards of information security with an enhanced approach that includes cognitive science.

Many organizations are doing some aspect of a "cogrisk" program but haven't formulated a complete framework; others have not even considered the possibility; and still others are on the path toward a functioning framework influenced by management. The Cognitive Risk Framework for Cybersecurity is in response to an interim process of transitioning to a new level of business operations (cognitive computing) informed by better intelligence to solve the problems that hinder growth.

New technologies (social media, communication channels, etc.) are changing how we think, work, entertain ourselves, and communicate on a global scale. These same technologies have created risks that were not imagined possible at their inception. As more advanced cognitive solutions come online in the near future cybersecurity professionals need a transitional plan and framework for managing in this new environment that is sustainable and adaptable as new solutions are introduced. If the consensus is that the human is the "weakest link" then we need tools to strengthen this vulnerability as well. The Cognitive Risk Framework for Cybersecurity is one approach to facilitate the transition to a more intuitive security program through its "guiding principles and five pillars."

References

Chen, H. and Xu, J., "Intelligence and Security Informatics." *Annual Review of Information Science and Technology* 40, 2006, 229–289.

Cybenko, G., Giani, A., Thompson, P., Cognitive Hacking: Advances in Computers, Department of Defense, Air Force Office of Scientific Research, Defense Advanced Research Projects Agency, the Office of Justice Programs, National Institute of Justice and Department of Justice award, 2003.

Douglas, M. and Wildavsky, A. B., *Risk and Culture: An Essay on the Selection of Technical and Environmental Dangers*. University of California Press, Berkeley, 1982.

Finucane, M. L., Slovic, P., Mertz, C. K., Flynn, J., and Satterfield, T. A., "Gender, Race, Perceived Risk: The 'White Male' Effect." *Health, Risk, & Society* 2, 2000, 159–172.

Fischhoff, B., Slovic, P., Lichtenstein, S., Read, S., and Combs, B., "How Safe is Safe Enough? A Psychometric Study of Attitudes Towards Technological Risks and Benefits." *Policy Sciences* 9, 1978, 127–152.

Flynn, J., Slovic, P., and Mertz, C. K., "Gender, Race, and Perception of Environmental Health Risk." *Risk Analysis* 14 (6), 1994, 1101–1108. Blackwell Publishing Ltd, 1539–6924.

Kahneman, D. and Tversky, A., "Prospect Theory: An Analysis of Decision under Risk." *Econometrica* 47 (2), March 1979, 263–291.

Slovic, P., "Perception of Risk." *Science* 236, 1987, 280–285.

Slovic, P., "Trust, Emotion, Sex, Politics, and Science: Surveying the Risk-Assessment Battlefield." *Risk Analysis* 19 (4), 1999, 689–701. Originally published in M. H. Bazerman, D. M. Messick, A. E. Tenbrunsel, and K. A. Wade-Benzoni (Eds.), Environment, ethics, and behavior (pp. 277–313). San Francisco: New Lexington, 1997. Revised version in The University of Chicago Legal Forum, 1997, 59–99.

Slovic, P., Lichtenstein, S., and Fischhoff, B., "Modeling the Societal Impact of Fatal Accidents." *Management Science* 30 (4), 1984, 464–474.

Slovic, P., Peters, E., Finucane, M. L., and MacGregor, D. G., "Affect, Risk, and Decision Making." *Health Psychology* 24 (4 Suppl), July 2005, S35–S40.

Slovic, P. and Weber, E. U., "Perception of Risk Posed by Extreme Events." Paper prepared for discussion at the conference "Risk Management Strategies in an Uncertain World." Palisades, New York, April 12–13, 2002.

Starr, C., "Social Benefit versus Technological Risk." *Science* 165, 1969, 1232–1238.

Sweller, J., "Cognitive Load during Problem Solving: Effects on Learning." *Cognitive Science* 12 (2), June 1988, 257–285.

Tversky, A. and Kahneman, D., "The Quarterly." *Journal of Economics* 106 (4), November 1991, 1039–1061.

Weber, E. U. and Milliman, R., "Perceived Risk Attitudes: Relating Risk Perception to Risky Choice." *Management Science* 43, 1997, 122–143.

Wildavsky, A., "No Risk is the Highest Risk of All." *American Scientist* 67, 1979, 32–37.

Bibliography

Prologue

http://www.huffingtonpost.com/2014/03/11/dianne-feinstein-cia_n
_4941352.html

Introduction

http://www.internetsociety.org/internet/what-internet/history-internet/brief
-history-internet
http://www.isoc.org/internet/history/brief.html
http://gilc.org/privacy/survey/intro.html
http://www.informationshield.com/intprivacylaws.html
https://en.wikipedia.org/wiki/History_of_cryptography
https://webfoundation.org/
https://brightplanet.com/2014/03/clearing-confusion-deep-web-vs-dark
-web/
https://www.torproject.org/about/sponsors.html.en

Chapter 1

http://eval.symantec.com/mktginfo/enterprise/white_papers/b-whitepaper
_exec_summary_internet_security_threat_report_xiii_04-2008.en-us
.pdf

http://www.computerweekly.com/news/4500273520/Encrypted-traffic
-security-analysis-a-top-priority-for-2016-says-Dell-Security

http://www.reuters.com/article/cybersecurity-routers-cisco-systems-upda-id
USL5N11L0VM20150915

http://uk.reuters.com/article/us-cybersecurity-routers-cisco-systems-idUK
KCN0RF0N420150915

http://www.bloomberg.com/news/articles/2016-06-23/the-right-to-be-for
gotten-and-other-cyberlaw-cases-go-to-court

http://www.algosec.com/en/resources/examining_the_dangers_of_complexity
_in_network_security_environments

http://www.pnas.org/content/102/41/14497.full, PNAS 2005 102 (41)
14497–14502; published ahead of print October 4, 2005, doi:10.1073
/pnas.0501426102

http://www.maths.adelaide.edu.au/matthew.roughan/Papers/PNAS_2005
.pdf

http://www.maoz.com/~dmm/talks/I2_member_meeting_2013.pdf

http://www.defenseone.com/threats/2014/10/cyber-attack-will-cause-significant
-loss-life-2025-experts-predict/97688/

http://www.nytimes.com/2012/10/12/world/panetta-warns-of-dire-threat
-of-cyberattack.html?_r=0

http://www.reuters.com/article/2015/07/30/us-usa-fbi-cyberattack
-idUSKCN0Q428220150730

http://www.bloomberg.com/news/articles/2015-04-22/in-the-dark-corners
-of-the-web-a-spider-intercepts-hackers

https://www.whitehouse.gov/the-press-office/2013/02/12/executive-order
-improving-critical-infrastructure-cybersecurity

https://people.eecs.berkeley.edu/~tygar/papers/Trust_in_Cyberspace.pdf

http://www.nap.edu/catalog/6161/trust-in-cyberspace

http://www.security-informatics.com/about

http://www.ists.dartmouth.edu/library/301.pdf

http://www.marketwatch.com/story/do-you-need-enterprise-grade-cyber
security-2015-09-21?dist=beforebell

http://www.npr.org/sections/alltechconsidered/2015/09/15/440252972
/when-cyber-fraud-hits-businesses-banks-may-not-offer-protection

https://www2.fireeye.com/WEB-2015RPTMaginotRevisited.html

Chapter 2

http://news.usni.org/2012/10/14/asymmetric-nature-cyber-warfare

https://en.wikipedia.org/wiki/Situation_awareness

https://en.wikipedia.org/wiki/Military_theory

https://en.wikipedia.org/wiki/The_Art_of_War

https://en.wikipedia.org/wiki/World_War_I

https://en.wikipedia.org/wiki/Situation_awareness#cite_note-20

http://ieeexplore.ieee.org/xpl/articleDetails.jsp?reload=true&arnumber=195097

https://en.wikipedia.org/wiki/Situation_awareness#cite_note-28

http://www.ists.dartmouth.edu/library/77.pdf reference for Libicki quote

https://www.schneier.com/crypto-gram/archives/2000/1015.html

http://www.nytimes.com/2014/01/18/business/a-sneaky-path-into-target
-customers-wallets.html?_r=2

http://www.bloomberg.com/bw/articles/2014-03-13/target-missed
-alarms-in-epic-hack-of-credit-card-data

https://www.uscg.mil/auxiliary/training/tct/chap5.pdf

http://www.usatoday.com/story/tech/news/2016/06/06/mark-zuckerbergs
-social-media-accounts-hacked/85477432/

http://citeseerx.ist.psu.edu/viewdoc/download?doi=10.1.1.87.6587&rep=rep1
&type=pdf

http://www.ists.dartmouth.edu/docs/ch.doc

http://dl.acm.org/citation.cfm?id=2500948

http://www.counterpane.com/crypto-gram-0010.html

https://www.washingtonpost.com/lifestyle/style/usaid-effort-to-under
mine-cuban-government-with-fake-twitter-another-anti-castro-fail
ure/2014/04/03/c0142cc0-bb75-11e3-9a05-c739f29ccb08_story.html

http://www.ists.dartmouth.edu/library/300.pdf

http://www.humanipo.com/news/37983/91-of-organisations-hit-by-cyber

http://isi2015.wixsite.com/isi-2015

https://duckduckgo.com/?q=cybersecurity+associations&t=ffab

https://duckduckgo.com/?q=university+associated+cyber+security+initiatives
&t=ffab

http://fortune.com/2016/04/12/facebook-chat-bots-messenger-app/

http://www.securityweek.com/next-big-cybercrime-vector-social-media

http://www.securityweek.com/iranian-sponsored-hackers-hit-critical-infra
structure-companies-research

http://www.securityweek.com/iranian-hackers-targeted-us-officials-elaborate
-social-media-attack-operation

http://research.google.com/pubs/ArtificialIntelligenceandMachineLearning
.html

https://www.technologyreview.com/s/601139/how-google-plans-to-solve
-artificial-intelligence/

http://www.techrepublic.com/article/how-googles-ai-breakthroughs-are
-putting-us-on-a-path-to-narrow-ai/

http://thehackernews.com/2016/04/artificial-intelligence-cyber-security.html

https://ccdcoe.org/publications/2011proceedings/ArtificialIntelligenceInCyber
Defense-Tyugu.pdf

https://securelist.com/analysis/publications/36325/cyber-expert-artificial
-intelligence-in-the-realms-of-it-security/

http://artificialtimes.com/blog/why-should-we-care-part-1/

https://www.helpnetsecurity.com/2016/06/02/ransomware-boss-earns-90000/

http://www.pcworld.com/article/2362980/russian-mobile-banking-trojan
-gets-ransomware-features-starts-targeting-us-users.html

https://polytechnic.purdue.edu/profile/rogersmk

http://arstechnica.com/security/2014/09/dyre-malware-branches-out-from
-banking-adds-corporate-espionage/

Chapter 3

http://www.nytimes.com/2015/09/26/world/asia/xi-jinping-white-house
.html?_r=0

http://www.chinadaily.com.cn/cndy/2011-09/14/content_13680896.htm

http://www.reuters.com/article/us-usa-cyber-ransomware-idUSKCN0X917X

http://www.cio.com/article/2415352/outsourcing/outsourcing--brazil-blos
soms-as-it-services-hub.html

http://www.nytimes.com/2015/12/01/technology/in-a-global-market-for
-hacking-talent-argentines-stand-out.html?_r=0

http://www.bloomberg.com/features/2016-how-to-hack-an-election/

http://breakinggov.com/2012/05/14/cyber-intelligence-sharing-intelligence
-with-infrastructure-pro/

http://www.eweek.com/security/the-paradox-of-todays-internet-and-cyber
-security-2.html

https://en.wikipedia.org/wiki/Alert_state; http://www.fbi.gov/news/news_blog
/director-discusses-encryption-patriot-act-provisions

https://en.wikipedia.org/wiki/Amos_Tversky;   https://en.wikipedia.org/wiki
/Daniel_Kahneman

https://hbr.org/2006/01/a-brief-history-of-decision-making

http://courses.washington.edu/pbafhall/514/514%20Readings/TimidChoices
AndBoldForecasts.pdf

http://www.eweek.com/security/the-paradox-of-todays-internet-and-cyber
-security.html

http://www.businessinsider.com/the-opm-breachs-cybersecurity-paradox
-2015-6

http://www.slate.com/articles/technology/technology/2012/05/malware_and
_computer_viruses_they_ve_left_porn_sites_for_religious_sites_.html

http://www.pwc.com/gx/en/issues/cyber-security/information-security-survey
.html

https://www.isc2cares.org/uploadedFiles/wwwisc2caresorg/Content/2013
-ISC2-Global-Information-SecurityWorkforce-Study.pdf

http://link.springer.com/referenceworkentry/10.1007%2F978-1-4419
-5906-5_774

https://en.wikipedia.org/wiki/Biba_Model

https://en.wikipedia.org/wiki/Clark%E2%80%93Wilson_model

http://csrc.nist.gov/cyberframework/rfi_comments/040813_forrester
_research.pdf

http://www.cisco.com/c/dam/en_us/solutions/industries/docs/gov
/cybersecurity_bvr_wp.pdf

http://newsbusters.org/blogs/joseph-rossell/2015/02/26/fcc-passes
-regulations-enabling-government-micromanage-internet

http://www.govtech.com/opinion/Cybersecuritys-Weakest-Link-Humans
.html

http://www.developer.com/tech/article.php/640831/Net-Present-Value-of
-Information-Security-Part-I.htm

http://urgentcomm.com/blog/attraction-and-training-keys-developing
-cybersecurity-talent

http://newsbusters.org/blogs/joseph-rossell/2015/02/26/fcc-passes
-regulations-enabling-government-micromanage-internet

https://www.whitehouse.gov/net-neutrality

https://www.fcc.gov/general/open-internet

http://www.nytimes.com/interactive/2015/07/29/technology/personaltech
/what-parts-of-your-information-have-been-exposed-to-hackers-quiz
.html?_r=0

https://en.wikipedia.org/wiki/Internet_governance

https://www.w3.org/support/

https://www.w3.org/Consortium/mission

http://www.nationaldefensemagazine.org/archive/2011/June/Pages/Whois
ResponsibleforCybersecurity.aspx

http://www.bloomberg.com/features/2016-labmd-ftc-tiversa/

http://www.bloomberg.com/news/articles/2013-03-05/protecting-privacy
-on-the-internet

https://www.ftc.gov/about-ftc/what-we-do/enforcement-authority

http://www.infoworld.com/article/2983774/security/attackers-go-on-malware
-free-diet.html

https://en.wikipedia.org/wiki/Cognitive_dissonance

http://journalsweb.org/siteadmin/upload/56864%20IJRET014045.pdf

https://en.wikipedia.org/wiki/Intertemporal_choice

https://dash.harvard.edu/bitstream/handle/1/4554332/Laibson_Intertemporal
Choice.pdf

https://www.invincea.com/2016/03/cyberedge-group-2016-cyberthreat
-defense-report/

Chapter 4

http://fortune.com/2015/04/24/data-breach-cost-estimate-dispute/

http://fortune.com/2015/03/27/how-much-do-data-breaches-actually-cost
-big-companies-shockingly-little/

http://www.ponemon.org/blog/a-few-challenges-in-calculating-total-cost
-of-a-data-breach-using-insurance-claims-payment-data

https://www.gfmag.com/magazine/may-2013/cover-growing-threat-the
-untold-costs-of-cybersecurity-

http://www.csoonline.com/article/2844133/data-protection/chertoff-cyber
security-takes-teamwork.html

http://www.rand.org/pubs/research_reports/RR610.html

http://www.theguardian.com/world/2016/mar/29/microsoft-tay-tweets
-antisemitic-racism

http://www.dailydot.com/technology/tor-botnet-microsoft-malware-remove/

http://www.reuters.com/article/net-us-citadel-botnet-idUSBRE9541
KO20130605

http://investors.proofpoint.com/releasedetail.cfm?ReleaseID=819799

http://www.gartner.com/smarterwithgartner/top-10-security
-predictions-2016/
http://www.eweek.com/security/idc-analysts-identify-it-security-trends-at
-rsa.html
http://www.informationweek.com/government/cybersecurity/defense
-department-adopts-nist-security-standards/d/d-id/1127706
http://nvlpubs.nist.gov/nistpubs/Legacy/SP/nistspecialpublication800-30r1
.pdf

Chapter 5

https://www.csiac.org/journal-article/cyber-deception/
http://www4vip.inl.gov/icis/deception/deception-used-for-cyber-defense.pdf
http://www.networkworld.com/article/3019760/network-security/the-ins
-and-outs-of-deception-for-cyber-security.html
https://ccdcoe.org/tallinn-manual.html
https://www.fbi.gov/about-us/investigate/cyber
https://www.dhs.gov/sites/default/files/publications/Law%20Enforcement
%20Cyber%20Incident%20Reporting.pdf
http://www.csg.org/knowledgecenter/docs/Misc0504Terrorism.pdf
http://www.gao.gov/new.items/d07705.pdf
http://www.gao.gov/assets/670/667512.pdf
http://www.gao.gov/products/GAO-15-6
http://www.bloomberg.com/news/articles/2016-05-19/u-s-can-t-detect
-when-cyber-attacks-are-under-way-survey-finds
http://archives.republicans.foreignaffairs.house.gov/112/Seg041511.pdf
https://ccdcoe.org/cycon/2013/proceedings/d2r1s7_boothby.pdf
http://www.cse.wustl.edu/~jain/cse571-14/ftp/cyber_espionage/
http://www.defense.gov/News-Article-View/Article/604466
https://www.blackhat.com/us-14/training/active-defense-offensive-counter
measures-and-hacking-back.html
https://ctovision.com/darpas-cyber-tools-we-have-had-our-hands-on-darpas
-distribution-platform-for-cyber-defense-tools/
https://www.dhs.gov/science-and-technology/csd-mtd
https://www.nitrd.gov/
https://www.whitehouse.gov/sites/default/files/microsites/ostp/fed_cyber
security_rd_strategic_plan_2011.pdf

Chapter 6

http://www.bloomberg.com/news/articles/2016-09-14/russia-says
-there-s-no-proof-it-hacked-sports-stars-health-data
http://www.bloomberg.com/politics/articles/2016-09-14/leaked-colin
-powell-emails-show-loathing-for-trump
http://www.ists.dartmouth.edu/library/301.pdf

http://www.pnnl.gov/cogInformatics/

https://www.nist.gov/news-events/news/2014/02/nist-releases-cyber
    security-framework-version-10

http://www.rff.org/files/sharepoint/Documents/Events/Workshops%20
    and%20Conferences/Climate%20Change%20and%20Extreme%20
    Events/slovic%20extreme%20events%20final%20geneva.pdf

https://en.wikipedia.org/wiki/Satisficing

https://en.wikipedia.org/wiki/Homo_economicus

https://en.wikipedia.org/wiki/Cognitive_load

https://en.wikipedia.org/wiki/The_Paradox_of_Choice

https://securityintelligence.com/cognitive-security-helps-beat-the-bad-guys
    -at-unprecedented-scale-and-speed/

http://www.ucalgary.ca/icic/files/icic/2-IJCINI-4101-CI&CC.pdf

https://en.wikipedia.org/wiki/Human%E2%80%93computer_interaction

https://ergoweb.com/what-is-cognitive-ergonomics/

http://www.dtic.mil/doctrine/new_pubs/jp2_0.pdf

http://www.americanbar.org/publications/law_practice_magazine/2013/july
    -august/cybersecurity-law-firms.html

http://thelawdictionary.org/best-efforts/

http://www.heatherlench.com/wp-content/uploads/2008/07/slovic.pdf

https://www.americanexpress.com/us/small-business/openforum/articles
    /guru-review-thinking-fast-and-slow/

http://www.ldeo.columbia.edu/chrr/documents/meetings/roundtable/white
    _papers/slovic_wp.pdf

http://www.skidmore.edu/~hfoley/Exp.Labs/Lab%203.S06/Slovic_2005.pdf

http://www.swarthmore.edu/SocSci/bschwar1/Choice%20Chapter.Revised
    .pdf

http://fas.org/irp/doddir/dod/jp2_0.pdf

http://definitions.uslegal.com/b/best-efforts/

Index

Page numbers with f refer to figures.

A

ABA Cybersecurity Handbook, 160
Ablon, Lillian, 106
Active Defense Harbinger
       Distribution (ADHD), 129
Advanced persistent threat (APT)
       attacks, 20–21
Apple, viii, xviii, 13, 43, 49–50,
       60–64, 77
Artificial Intelligence (AI)
   "big four" risks of, 53–54
   general AI, 50
   machine learning and, 88–89,
       113–114, 134, 145–147
   narrow AI, 50
   search engines and, 108
   strong AI, 50
   types of, 40–42, 45, 49–56
   weak AI, 50
Art of War, The, 25
Ashley Madison, 1–4
Asymmetrical intelligence, 157

Auerbach, David, 71
Autonomous attack, 52–54, 122
Avid Life Media, 2–3
Azzopardi, Myrna, 123

B

Bank of America, 56
Banks
   cyberattacks on, 54–56, 60
   cyber intelligence for, 63
   data breaches in, 30–35,
       110–111
   fraudulent activity in, 12–13,
       17–18
   phishing attempts on, 75
Becker, Gary S., 135
Bell-LaPadula Model, 73
Berners-Lee, Tim, vii, xix, xxii, 81
Bernoulli, Daniel, 67
"Best efforts" considerations, 145,
       160–162
Biba Integrity Model, 73

Biba, Kenneth J., 73
Biderman, Noel, 2–3
Big data analytics, 53–54
"Big Four" risks, 53–54; *see also*
    Artificial Intelligence
Black Hat Conference, 65
Black market, viii–xiv, 59–60,
    106–116, 125–128, 157
BlackPOS malware, 29–31
Black's Law Dictionary, 160
Blindness, inattentional, 48, 71
Blindness, risk, 85–86
"Bounded rationality" theory, 67,
    133, 143
Boyd, John, 25–26
Boyd Loop, 26, 28–29
Boyer, Wayne F., 120
Bring Your Own Device (BYOD),
    46, 84, 105

C

Caputo, Deanna D., 67
Chertoff, Michael, 105–106
Christiansen, Chris, 112
CIA, viii, 44, 53
Cisco Systems, 4–5, 47
Cisco Systems Trust Model, 74, 75
Clark–Wilson Integrity Model,
    73–74
Cloud computing, xviii, 6, 11, 56,
    86, 111
Cognitive behavior
    cybersecurity and, viii, 21, 23–57,
        89–97, 150, 161
    role of, 21
    situational awareness and, 23–57
    vulnerability and, viii
Cognitive computing, viii, 150, 161;
    see also Cognitive behavior
Cognitive defense strategies, xiii, 59,
    96–97
Cognitive dissonance theory, 85–86

Cognitive hacking
    concept of, 35–37
    defensive strategies for, 38
    defining, xiii, 17, 35
    semantic attacks and, 24–25
    study of, 33–35
    technology and, 14–17
    types of, 134
Cognitive informatics, 33–34,
    134–135, 144–145, 144f,
    150–152
Cognitive load, 48, 67–71, 145–148
Cognitive models, 154–155
Cognitive risk enhancements, 94–95
Cognitive Risk Framework for
        Cybersecurity (CRFC)
    cognitive informatics security,
        145, 150–152
    cognitive risk governance, 145,
        152–156
    concept of, 133–134
    cybersecurity intelligence and,
        145, 156–160
    intentional controls design,
        145–149
    internal controls for, 133–162
    legal "best efforts" considerations,
        145
    minimizing risk, 128–129
    options in, 113–114
    pillars of, 76–77, 143, 144f,
        145–162
    requirements for, 76–77, 108
    risk management for, 133–162
    security informatics, 145,
        150–152
Cognitive risk governance, 145,
    152–156
Cognitive risk management, viii, xi,
    xiv, 91–92, 134, 151
Cognitive risk program, 24,
    42–43, 114, 140–144,
    151, 161

Cognitive science, 43, 89–97, 134,
	150, 161; *see also* Cognitive
	behavior
Cognitive security
	cognitive informatics and,
		150–152
	explanation of, 38–43, 150–151
	integration of, 114
	solutions for, 158
	tools for, 91
Cognitive Security (CogSec), viii, ix,
	xiv, 33, 38, 141
Comey, James, 64
Continuous monitoring, 25–26, 26f,
	117
Counterterrorism, 39, 41, 126
Cross-site scripting (XSS) attack, 2
Cyber and Data Security Handbook,
	160
Cyber armistice, 59
Cyberattacks
	artificial intelligence and, 50–54
	autonomous attack, 52–54, 122
	black markets and, 106–116
	clearinghouse for, 6, 31–32
	data breaches, 30–35, 90, 101–102,
		110–111, 133–134
	defense strategies for, 92–98
	espionage and, 5–7, 61–64,
		122–129
	hackers and, vii–ix, xiii–xix
	malware attacks, 29–33, 54–55,
		59–60
	phishing attacks, xiii, 29–30, 38,
		46–47, 75, 127
	proliferation of, 44–45, 71
	reporting, 32–33
	risk and, 60, 65–66, 84–86
	risk management for, 133–136
	situational awareness and, 21,
		23–57
	on "soft" targets, ix, xiii, 5,
		107–111
	on Target, 29–33
	vulnerability and, 69–71, 74–77
Cyber black market, viii–xiv, 59–60,
	106–116, 125–128, 157
Cybercrime
	hackers and, vii–ix, xiii–xiv,
		xxi–xxii
	minimizing, 115–116
	victims of, 32, 36, 47, 54, 62, 75,
		92, 98, 115–116
Cyber espionage, 5–7, 61–64, 116,
	122–129
Cyber extortion, 54, 59, 82–83,
	89
Cyber Fast Track (CFT), 129
Cyber hostility, 53
Cyber intelligence, 47, 62–63, 89,
	151, 158–162
Cyber intrusions, 59, 124, 133–134,
	150, 161
Cyber paradox, 59–99, 110, 126,
	133–134, 155
Cybersecurity
	cognitive behavior and, viii, 21,
		23–57, 89–97, 150, 161
	cognitive risk framework,
		133–162
	deception and, 119–132
	defense strategies, xiv, 13–14, 92,
		130–131, 143–145, 144f,
		155–162
	espionage and, 5–7, 61–64, 116,
		122–129
	hacker mind and, 119–132
	internal controls for, 133–162
	moving target defense, 130–131
	risk management for, viii,
		133–162
	situational awareness and, 21,
		23–57
	skeptics on, 70–71
	skills for, 7–8, 41–42, 55–70,
		106–109

studies on, 8, 14 22, 38–43,
60–64, 67–68, 72–73,
136–137
vulnerability and, viii, xvii–xviii,
xxii, 1–22
weighing threats, 101–117
Cybersecurity intelligence, 145,
156–160
Cybersecurity Intelligence and
Defense Strategies (CIDS),
155–159
Cyberthreat Defense Report, 92,
96–97
Cyber trust, 14–18, 74; *see also*
Trustworthiness
Cyberwarfare, xiii, 23–28, 55,
59–66, 119–125

D

Darknets, viii, 110
Dark web, xx–xxi, 12, 59, 111
DARPA, xv, xix, 14,
128–129
Data breaches, 30–35, 90, 101–102,
110–111, 133–134
Datapocalypse, 53–54
Data Protection Act, xvii
Daugherty, Michael, 82–83
Davis, Richard, 63
Deception
cybersecurity and, 119–132
defensive strategies for, xiv,
121–122, 128–131
detection of, 17, 39, 51, 91,
119–122, 126, 131
growth of, 119
hacker mind and, 119–132
Decision theory, 134–135
Decoy method, 121
Deep learning, 50–51
Deep web, xx–xxi, 21, 54
DEFCON, 65

Defense Advanced Research
Projects Agency (DARPA),
xv, xix, 14, 128–129
Defense strategies
cognitive defense strategies, xiii,
59, 96–97
cyber defense strategies, xiv,
13–14, 92–98, 130–131,
143–145, 144f, 155–162
Dell, 4, 84
Denial-of-service (DDoS) attacks,
111, 123
Department of Homeland Security,
32, 42, 105, 124–125, 130,
151
Design-Basis Threat, 125
Discount factors, 87, 90
Dissimulation, 120–121
Doyle, John, 9, 19, 78
Drones, xviii, 18, 111

E

eCommerce, vii, xviii, 6, 16, 45,
76–77, 81, 107–108,
116–117
Econometrica, 66
Efficiency component, 9
Einstein, Albert, 105
Electronic Crime Task Forces
(ECTFs), 124
Electronic Fund Transfer Act, 18
Emulex, 37
Encryption methods, vii–viii,
xvii–xviii, 55–56, 64, 74,
156
Endowment effect, 93–95
Espionage, 5–7, 61–64, 116, 122–129
Evolvability, 10

F

Facebook, 34, 45, 60, 108, 148

Fan Hui, 50
FBI, viii, xxi, 12, 43, 54, 64, 75–77,
        109–111, 115, 124
Federal Communications
        Commission (FCC), xviii,
        77–78
Federal Reserve, 105, 116
Federal Trade Commission Act,
        82
Federal Trade Commission (FTC),
        82–83, 125
Feinstein, Diane, viii
Financial Services Information
        Sharing and Analysis
        Center (FS-ISAC), 63
Financial Services Modernization
        Act, xvii
FireEye, 4, 19–22, 30
Four Horsemen of Datapocalypse,
        53–54
Fund Transfer Act, 18

G

"Galactic Network," xv
Game theory, 50, 130
Global Internet Liberty Campaign
        (GILC), xvi
GoDaddy, 47
Go games, 50–51
Golay, Andrea A., 106
Gonzalez, Albert, 32
Google, xx, 6, 40, 45, 49–50, 55,
        60–62, 108, 148
Gordon, Lawrence, 104
Gorman, Sara, 139
Government agency hacks, 11–12
Gramm–Leach–Bliley Act (GLBA),
        xvii

H

Hackers

cognitive hacking by, xiii, 14–17,
        24–25, 35
conferences on, 60, 65
cybercrime and, vii–ix, xiii–xiv,
        xxi–xxii
deception and, 119–132
decoy methods, 121
dissimulation methods, 120–121
first reports of, xxi–xxii
of government agencies, 11–12
greatest numbers of, 60
malware attacks, 29–33
masking methods, 120–121
mimicking methods, 120–121
mind of, 119–132
tactics of, 20–21
tricks of, 20–21
"Hacker's Bazaar, The," 106–107,
        109–110, 114
"Hard" targets, ix, 107–108, 111
Homeland Security, 32, 42, 105,
        124–125, 130, 151
Human–machine interactions, viii,
        xiii, 38, 42, 48, 81, 94–96,
        114, 126, 155–158

I

Immigration and Customs
        Enforcement Homeland
        Security Investigations
        (ICE HSI), 124
Impact Team, 1–3
Inattentional blindness, 48, 71
Information Sharing and Analysis
        Center (ISAC), 63
Institute of Electrical and
        Electronics Engineers
        (IEEE), xviii, 41
Integrity models, 73–74
Intelligence and Security Informatics
        (ISI), viii, xiv, 16–17, 33, 35,
        38–39, 41, 151

Intelligence gathering, 55, 127,
 157–159
Intelligence sharing, 31–32, 63
Intentional controls design, 145–149
Interagency Security Committee
 (ISC), 125
*International Journal of Cognitive
 Informatics and Natural
 Intelligence*, 150
Internet Corporation for Assigned
 Names and Numbers
 (ICANN), 79
Internet Engineering Task Force
 (IETF), 79
Internet of Things (IoT), xviii,
 18, 53, 63, 85, 105–106,
 111–113
Internet support network, 79–81,
 80f
Internetworking architecture, xvi, xix
Intertemporal choice, 87, 89–90
Intrusion detection, 161
Intrusion prevention system (IPS)
 attacks, 4

J

Jacob, Mark, 37
Jacobs, Jay, 101
Jobs, Steve, 13–14, 49

K

Kahneman, Daniel, 28, 66–67, 135,
 142, 143, 153
Kleinrock, Leonard, xvi

L

Landwehr, Carl, 35
Lean approach, 94–95
Legal "best efforts" considerations,
 145, 160–162

Libicki, Martin C., 28, 44, 106
Licklider, J. C. R., xv, xxii
LinkedIn, 34, 44, 47, 65
Loeb, Martin, 104
Loss aversion, 90, 93–95, 142–143

M

Machine learning
 algorithms for, 40
 artificial intelligence and, 88–89,
  113–114, 134, 145–147
 challenges of, 49
 types of, 40
Maginot's Line, 19–21, 23
Magna Carta, xix
Malvertisement, 21, 38, 71, 134
Malware attacks; *see also*
  Cyberattacks
 proliferation of, 44–45, 71
 ransomware, 54–55, 59–60
 reporting, 32–33
 on Target, 29–33
Malware concentration, 20–22,
 21f
Masking methods, 120–121
McQueen, Miles A., 120
Mental models, 27, 29
Microsoft, 40–41, 45, 111
Military theory, 25
Miller, Judy, 160
Mimicking method, 120–121
Mobile devices, xviii, 11, 18, 44, 81,
 96–97, 110, 147–148, 156
Modularity component, 9–10
Morganstern, Oskar, 67
Moss, Jeff, 65
Moving target defense, 130–131
Mueller, Robert, 75

N

National Cash Register (NCR), xviii

National Cybersecurity and Communications Integration Center (NCCIC), 124
National Institute of Standards and Technology (NIST), 13, 25, 26f, 117, 136
National Security Agency, 44
National Security Council, 126
National Telecommunications and Information Administration (NTIA), 79
Netanyahu, Binyamin, 64
Netflix, 148
Net Neutrality, 77–78
Networked Information Systems (NIS), 14–16
Networking and Information Technology Research and Development (NITRD), 130–131

O

Obama, Barack, xx, 59, 63, 78
OODA Loop, 26, 28–29
"Open Internet," vii, xv–xx, 78, 84
Operational intelligence, 157
Operation Cleaver, 46–47
Optimal outcomes, 69–70, 87–91, 137–143, 154–155

P

Page, Larry, 6
Pai, Ajit, 78
Panetta, Leon, 11
Paradox of Choice, The, 84, 149
PayPal, 47
Peña Nieto, Enrique, 61
Pervasive computing, 53
Pfleeger, Shari Lawrence, 43, 44, 67

Phishing attacks, xiii, 29–30, 38, 46–47, 75, 127
Privacy rights, viii, xv, xix
Prospect theory, 28, 66–67, 143

R

Ransomware, 54–55, 59–60
Rationality, bounded, 67, 133, 143
"Rational man" theory, 67, 143
Reinforcement learning, 40; *see also* Machine learning
Reliability component, 9
Rishikof, Harvey, 160
Risk analysis, 139–140
Risk awareness, 77, 115, 142
Risk blindness, 85–86
Risk deafness, 56, 66, 85–86
Risk management, viii, xi, xiv, 7–8, 86, 91–92, 133–162
Risk perception, 137–142
Robust Yet Fragile (RYF) concept, 9–11, 10f, 19, 78
Rogers, Marcus, 56

S

"Satisficing," 137–138
Scalability component, 9
Schneier, Bruce, 23, 36
Schwartu, Win, 11
Schwartz, Barry, 84, 149
Search engines, xx, 83, 108
Secret Service, 124
Secure Socket Layer (SSL), xvii, 56
Securities and Exchange Commission (SEC), 18, 32
Security analysts, 8, 25, 31, 46–49, 62–63, 69–71, 148–150
Security breaches, 18–19, 20–22, 31–33, 88–90, 113
Security control systems, 3, 47, 88, 121–122, 145, 148–149

Security informatics, 145, 150–152
Segal, Adam, 126
Semantic attacks
    cognitive hacking and, 24–25
    concept of, 35
    countermeasures to, 35–36
    explanation of, 35–36
    proliferation of, 44, 47–48
    study of, 17
    types of, 28, 37–38
Semisupervised learning, 40; *see also*
    Machine learning
Sensemaking, 27, 29
Sepúlveda, Andrés, 61–62
Simon, Herbert A., 67, 134–135,
    137, 143
Situational assessment, 26–27, 29
Situational awareness
    advances in, 23–57
    cyberattacks and, 21, 23–57
    explanation of, 25–28, 26f
    role of, 21
Situational understanding, 29
Slovic, Paul, 135–137, 139–141, 143
SLTT law enforcement, 124–125
Smart appliances, 111–112, 147
Smartphones, viii, 43, 49, 64, 77–78,
    84, 93, 97, 148
Smart systems, xv, 14–17, 34, 91–92,
    145
Snowden, Edward, 44
"Soft" targets, ix, xiii, 5, 107–111
Spear-phishing attacks, xiii,
    29–30, 38, 47, 127; *see also*
    Phishing attacks
Spider intercepts, 12–13
Spitler, Marc, 101
Spying tools, 5; *see also* Espionage
Starr, C., 139
Status quo, 93–95, 146–147
Strategic intelligence, 157
Stringer, Simon, 50, 51
Sun Tzu, 25, 119

Supervised learning, 40; *see also*
    Machine learning
Surface web, xx–xxi
Sweller, John, 145, 147
"SYNful Knock" hack, 4–5, 7

T

Tactical intelligence, 157
Tail risks, 44, 87, 105, 153
*Tallinn Manual on the Law of Cyber
    Warfare*, 122, 127
Target stores, 29–33
Terrorist activity, 39–40, 124
Terrorist attacks, viii, 64, 77
Thompson, Paul, 35
Thompson, Wayne, 40
Three Mile Island accident,
    155–156
Thurman, James, 65
TOR network, xx–xxi, 109, 111
Transportation networks, 47
Trust models, 45, 74–77, 89
Trustworthiness, xix, 14–22, 45–48,
    71–77, 89–91
Tversky, Amos, 28, 66–67, 142, 143,
    153
Twitter, 12–13, 36, 45
Tyugu, Enn, 52

U

United States Agency for
    International Development
    (USAID), 36–37
Unsupervised learning, 40; *see also*
    Machine learning
U. S. Bank, 63
Utility theory, 66, 87, 89

V

Verizon, 101–104

Von Neumann, John, 67
Vulnerability
  cognitive behavior and, viii
  corridor of, 77, 86, 89, 96
  cyberattacks and, 69–71, 74–77
  cybersecurity and, viii, xvii–xviii,
    xxii, 1–22
  management of, 69–71, 74–77
  risk and, 60, 65–66
  security controls for, 121

W

Warfare, 23–28, 62–66, 119–125;
    see also Cyberwarfare
Wheeler, Tom, 78
Wi-Fi access, xv, xviii
Wildavsky, A., 137, 140
Wireless devices, xviii, 11, 18, 44,
    96–97, 110, 147–148, 156
World Wide Web Consortium
    (W3C), 81

World Wide Web Foundation, vii,
    xix
Wormuth, Christine, 128

X

Xi Jinping, xx, 59

Y

Yahoo, xx
YouTube, 148

Z

Zatko, Peiter, 129
Zero-day threats, 61–62, 69, 107,
    111
Zero-Trust Model, 74; *see also*
    Trustworthiness
Zuckerberg, Mark, 34, 44–45
ZunZuneo, 36–37

Printed in the United States
by Baker & Taylor Publisher Services